Preaching What We Practice

Proclamation and Moral Discernment

Preaching What We Practice

Proclamation and Moral Discernment

David J. Schlafer

Timothy F. Sedgwick

MOREHOUSE PUBLISHING

Harrisburg, Pennsylvania

Unless otherwise noted, the Scripture quotations contained herein are from the New Revised Standard Version Bible, copyright © 1989 by the Division of Christian Education of the National Council of Churches of Christ in the U.S.A. Used by permission. All rights reserved.

Ellen Davis's sermon, "And in Him All Things Hold Together," is reprinted with permission from the *Virginia Seminary Journal* (December 1977): 2–5.

Marianne Budde's sermon, "Harvesting to the Very Edges," is reprinted with permission from the *Virginia Seminary Journal* (July 2002): 43–46.

Morehouse Publishing, P.O. Box 1321, Harrisburg, PA 17105

Morehouse Publishing, 445 Fifth Avenue, New York, NY 10016

Morehouse Publishing is an imprint of Church Publishing Incorporated.

Cover design by Brenda Klinger

Library of Congress Cataloging-in-Publication Data

Schlafer, David, J., 1944–
    Preaching what we practice : proclamation and moral discernment / David J. Schlafer, Timothy F. Sedgwick.
      p. cm.
    Includes bibliographical references and index.
    ISBN 978-0-8192-2218-3 (pbk.)
    1. Preaching. 2. Christian ethics. 3. Discernment (Christian theology).
    4. Christian ethics—Sermons. 5. Discernment (Christian theology)—Sermons. 6. Sermons, American—21st century. I. Sedgwick, Timothy F.
    II. Title.
      BV4235.E75.S35 2007
      241—dc22
                                    2006102326

Printed in the United States of America

07 08 09 10 11 12   10 9 8 7 6 5 4 3 2 1

In gratitude and with respect for my teacher,
Arthur F. Holmes, and for his commitment,
with generations of students, to fostering the
integration of faith and learning
—*David J. Schlafer*

In thanks and with joy for my brother,
R. Stephen Sedgwick, and for our conversations
between pulpit and pew, priest and professor.
—*Timothy F. Sedgwick*

Contents

Acknowledgments

THE AUTHORS ARE DEEPLY GRATEFUL to the following preaching colleagues who have given permission for the use of their sermons in this book:

Kim Beckmann
Marianne Budde
Ellen Davis
Susan Gaumer
Anne Howard
Edward Probert

In addition to their commitments and skills as preachers, they give effective testimony to the assumption of this book: the work of preaching what we practice, while it can be modeled by individuals, can be embodied only in community.

Introduction

AFTER 9/11 AND THE TERRORIST DESTRUCTION of the Trade Center Towers in New York City and the southwest rim of the Pentagon in Washington, D.C., we asked each other if we had heard or seen any good sermons. In the years since those attacks, we have continued to ask the question: What is being preached?

On the Sunday after the firestorms, and for a few weeks thereafter, churches were full across the country. Congregations heard sermons that recalled the horror and offered strident words of judgment or reassuring words of hope (or perhaps a mix of both). But as weeks went on, we heard little that helped us make sense of violence, judgment and grace, conversion, forgiveness, love and justice, citizenship and discipleship, what God was calling us to do and to be, or what holiness and faithfulness might require in our time.

Perhaps more telling, we have heard few sustained explorations of these questions. Within weeks of 9/11, attendance was back to "normal"; the newcomers did not return. We wondered, one of us a Christian ethicist and the other a Christian homiletician, what was missing, what was needed, what would help in generating a kind of preaching from which listeners, old and new, could not stay away. What words from the pulpit might kindle a compelling desire to engage seriously the claims of Christian faith? Our broader concern: How do preachers move beyond once-told-tales of terror and often-intoned mantras of judgment, hope, and warning to fresh presentings of Christian faith as a way of life?

We continued to meet, sharing our concerns and convictions. In our unfolding discussions:

- We named some factors that make "moral discernment" preaching difficult.

- We framed a set of theses to capture what we felt was most deeply needed.

- We outlined a set of practices we regard as necessary wellsprings for disciplined Christian reflection and moral discernment in situations of crisis and quandary.

- We delineated some homiletical strategies preachers can employ in order to evoke discerning reflection and faithful action.

- We ruminated on how the lectionary cycles in the liturgical year might be used more effectively in the service of preaching moral discernment.

- We tried to translate our ideas into concrete "for instances": what such preaching might look, sound, feel like "on the ground."

- We dreamed about where long-term preaching intended to foster Christian moral discernment might lead preachers and congregations alike.

Through our interchanges, we have become more convinced of how critical it is for the church to preach moral discernment. In committing our ideas to writing, we hope to open and enlarge a discussion of what is needed, and to offer some resources for preaching that address moral crises in terms of Christian faith. To this end we have included sermons or parts of sermons so readers can hear what such preaching might "sound like."

Sermons are meant to be heard and don't always translate easily into written texts. Sermons are context specific, not only in content but also in rhetorical style. We have, therefore, sought some diversity in the sermons we have chosen. Still, our sermons are limited largely to mainline churches and mainstream congregations (i.e., we don't draw on sermons that would suggest what moral discernment preaching would sound like for a more marginalized or oppressed people). We also felt it only honest to include examples of our own attempts at preaching moral discernment.

We hope this book will focus minds and voices on how sermons can explore the Christian life in terms of particular quandaries addressed through a clear vision of the practices that constitute the Christian moral life. There are, of course, other purposes in preaching that are directly related to ethics: for example, prophetic denunciation, liberating vision, or call to action. Such purposes have their place and may be just what is called for in a particular community and in a particular time. But failing to preach moral discernment consistently can lead either to religious moralism or to a neglect of the faith we are called to practice.

As we began to write, one of us would draft a chapter and the other would revise. Back and forth we would go until we agreed on what we had to say and on our collective voice. To conceive and choreograph a duet is more difficult than to produce a solo performance—but, we believe, far richer. Certainly it has been so for our own learning, and so, we hope, it will be for you.

CHAPTER 1

Crisis and Quandary

THE TERRORIST ATTACKS OF 9/11 provoked a crisis. From American leaders, pundits, and citizens came a solemn refrain: "On this day, the world was changed forever." Those living in oft-invaded homelands might have questioned the sense of proportion implicit in the claim. Much of the world, however, was initially empathetic, knowing firsthand the tangled feelings of shock, violation, threat, and challenge that terrorism precipitates. Yet untangling such feelings was an essential task in the aftermath of 9/11. Much untangling work remains.

Katrina posed a different crisis. The 2005 category 5 hurricane flooded New Orleans and the Gulf Coast and swept away life as it was. Violence flared. People scattered. Relief efforts began. The politics of poverty and race were revealed. The long and arduous work of rebuilding and resettlement continues. National commentators spoke of a post-Katrina world, but whether Katrina marks a decisive moment of change remains to be seen.

Crisis is first defined by *The Oxford English Dictionary* (*OED*) as "the turning point of a disease that leads to recovery or death." A second definition follows: "a vitally important or decisive stage in the progress of anything, a turning point." *The Merriam-Webster Dictionary* shifts attention and gives primacy to a more contemporary (and more American) usage. It emphasizes not so much what a crisis is, as how it feels to those affected: "a paroxysmal attack of pain, distress, or disordered function." The distinction is instructive. The *OED* definitions imply the urgency of astute diagnosis; the *Merriam-Webster* entry implies a pressing need for palliative therapy: "Whatever it takes to stop the pain!" Both senses interplay in crisis situations; it is not easy to discern what is happening.

Responses in the wake of 9/11 were clearly called for, and decisions were made. The roads taken (as Robert Frost says) have "made all the difference," though many crossroads lie ahead and where roads already taken will ultimately lead is beyond our line of sight. Choices made by American leaders after 9/11 have left a legacy. Decisive actions undertaken as "clear responses to acts of terror" have produced political and moral situations more ambiguous and conflicted still. Reactivity has spread. Shrill "either/or" language has dramatically escalated in debates on national policy and on the consequences of electing this or that candidate for political office.

Emergency responders to Katrina lacked coordination. The people of New Orleans couldn't be evacuated. Deployment of National Guard units was late and violence escalated. Communications broke down. The natural disaster became a social disaster. Officials and pundits blamed past policies and present politics: failure in the construction of the flood levees, mismanagement of funds to update those levees, the destruction of the wetlands, failure to develop adequate emergency plans, inadequate funding, and cronyism and incompetence at the Federal Emergency Management Agency (FEMA) and at state and local governments. And while most agreed that the African-American residents of New Orleans suffered the ravages of the hurricane and its aftermath out of all proportion because they were poor, there was no agreement over who should do what.

It is tempting, in the midst of such crises, to give decision-making priority over deliberation. "We must do something!" often trumps "What's the matter? What is going on?" Resolution overcomes questioning. We declare, "God is on our side," and don't ask the questions, "Where is God? What is God calling us to do?" Deliberate processes of painstaking discernment are frequently disparaged as a "paralysis of analysis." Immediate responses to crises, however, often turn out to be instances of fools rushing in where angels fear to tread. So-called decisive actions can do more harm than good, especially in the long run. Bringing in all voices to develop consensus about how to rebuild New Orleans was impossible. But no developed plan—for what to condemn and what to tear down, what to rebuild and what not to build, and what to build entirely new—only means that past power brokers will be replaced with new ones. Still, endless deliberation and debate can produce serious negative consequences as well. Decisions have to be made. Similarly, refraining indefinitely from taking action to stem the tide of terrorism or failure to counteract the repression of civil rights imposed in the name of fighting terrorism—*either* could contribute to further fragility in both security and freedom.

The 9/11 crisis and Hurricane Katrina are graphic illustrations in the United States of many different moral situations wherein stakes are high, issues are conflicted, and pressures for resolution are intense.

- Conservative evangelicals press for a marriage amendment to the U.S. Constitution while meetings of Episcopal, Lutheran, Methodist, and Presbyterian churches debate whether gay and lesbian persons can serve as pastors, priests, or bishops.

- As covert forms of business practices come to light and companies crumble—marked most vividly by the collapse of Enron—there is more to face than the "paroxysms of pain" experienced by those who lose their jobs, their retirement benefits, or their investments. Serious questions must be raised concerning business practices and regulations.

- The fate of Terry Schiavo raises a national debate on whether food should be withdrawn from persons in a coma or a persistent vegetative state.

Terrorism, world hunger, the AIDS crisis, environmental protection versus economic development, criminalization or decriminalization of drug use, stem cell research, financing social security and public health care: crises threaten to overwhelm our ability to stop, question, and listen before we react or else simply withdraw and give the power of decision to someone else.

How do we make sense of what is happening? What are the ranges of possible response? As Christians we further need to ask, "Where is God? How should I respond so as to be faithful to God? What is the will of God for me?" How nice it would be if God could simply be appealed to as The Moral Answer Man! On the contrary, however, setting moral choice in a theological frame of reference almost always makes matters even more challenging.

How, then, do pastors, priests, and all those called to leadership in communities of Christian faith best serve their fellow seeking-believers who struggle to address their lives morally and theologically? Personal counseling, communal pastoral care, congregational development, continuing theological education, sacramental administration: all these are central to what has been called "the cure of souls." In these ways a congregational leader can help members stop and stand in the presence of God, listen, give voice to what is happening, recognize and identify possible courses of action, and support and sustain one another in the choices that are made.

In a community's quest for moral discernment, however, preachers have a particularly critical role. The preacher addresses the congregation each Sunday and at other times between, including special occasions. As preacher, the leader seeks to move between Scripture and our lives in order to "break open" the word of God that we might see God's grace and hear what God is calling us to be and to do. Central to this calling is addressing the community of faith as a moral community. This is a question for homiletics but one that requires homiletics to stay in lively conversation with ethics and moral theology.

Preachers are often cartooned as finger-waving, fist-pounding pontificators who inform and exhort their listeners in detail about what they should or shouldn't "be" or "do." The agenda of the finger-pointing preacher may be individual or corporate, the angle of vision "liberal" or "conservative"; but there stands the preacher in the pulpit "six feet above contradiction," a combination motivational speaker and moral authoritarian.

Alternatively, preachers are sometimes caricatured not so much as symbols of authoritarian influence as of abstract irrelevance. Up there in the lofty pulpit, the preacher is out of touch. The world is in crisis, yet the preacher dispenses only flower petals: theological propositions, finely parsed but vague, or sentimental pieties and platitudes, perfumed but musty.

It can hardly be surprising if preachers themselves are often "spooked" by such stereotypes. (Who really wants to be a tyrant or a bore?) It is also not surprising when, with no more nurture than many preachers have received for their critical role as mentors in moral discernment, they are at a loss as to what they should be about when they enter the pulpit.

On the Sunday after 9/11, churches were full of folks with glazed eyes, broken hearts, and eager ears, asking by their presence, "Is there a word from the Lord?" Not just a word of comfort or explanation but also a word to light a path across a landscape rendered suddenly terrifying and uncertain. Every bit as evident as the hopeful question in the initial presence of these many visitors was the pessimistic answer in their subsequent absence: "words, mere words." If preachers had better known what to say—and how—might it have made a difference? Might it yet?

It would be easy enough for an ethicist and a homiletician to issue their own pontifications or platitudes upon fellow theological professionals: "Shame on us!" "The whole problem is . . ." But the concerns described here are too critical for that. We need, together, as participants in a community of seeker-believers, to look discerningly at what it might mean to preach in conditions of moral crisis and quandary. The place to begin is with naming some of the reasons that preaching effectively toward moral discernment and formation in a faith community is such a demanding vocation. Why is the preacher's task so hard?

1. There are dynamics inherent in moral discernment that no single sermon can fully engage.

2. There are conditions at work in culture that render the task of preaching especially formidable.

3. There are factors in the life of the church that make it difficult for preachers to employ Scripture effectively.

1. DYNAMICS IN MORAL DISCERNMENT THAT NO SINGLE SERMON CAN FULLY ENGAGE

Moral decisions require a constant interplay between broad, overarching principles and the particular factors involved in a situation of actual choice

In trying to determine both what we should do and what is "right" or "best," we ask "Why?" as well as "What?" and "How?" We reflect on and seek reasons, rules, ideals, or goods to be affirmed or realized in the action we consider taking. We decide on the basis of our principles. Yet in our actual choices, we are not simply sorting situations into prefixed moral category bins. Before we ask, "Why?" we must ask, "What is happening? What is in conflict? What can be done?" And as always the devil is in the details.

Actions can plausibly be "read" in different, even conflicting ways. Going to war, for instance, can be seen as the sacrifice of life for liberty or as fear-driven, shortsighted self-interest. To some extent, such alternative readings are based on the availability or recognition of data. (The "justification" given for going to war in Iraq was that country's supposed possession of "weapons of mass destruction.") Yet "the facts" alone are seldom sufficient to ensure a common assessment. (There were many who, even assuming the presence of weapons of mass destruction, were opposed "on principle" to undertaking a preemptive war.)

Instead of simply offering moral ideals or giving specific directives, effective moral guidance from the pulpit must nurture the active process of moral reflection. It must foster interpretation of specific events in light of broader patterns of meaning. Preaching must mentor rather than tell. How does any speech, let alone a speech invoking "God's will," do that? Exploring together understandings, convictions, and assumptions seems central to moving from what *is* to what *ought* to be done. No single sermon is itself such a full conversation. How then, we must ask, can preaching, over time, nurture such thoughtful, faithful, and communal discussion?

Moral decision-making has to do with character as well as choice of action

We say, "You will know them by their fruit. A good tree produces good fruit." Or, we say of someone's actions, "That's in character." Be loving, kind, merciful, forgiving—these statements of character assume that persons have enduring attitudes, dispositions, and intentions, and that they act accordingly. Some ethical theorists (and more ordinary folks as well), recognizing this feature of moral experience, conclude that we can solve the questions of ethics by focusing primarily (or even exclusively) on character and character formation. But, of course, moral education and formation is itself complex. What we do expresses who we are, but what we do is not simply an extension of our character.

How should we understand terrorism or the problem of poverty in America? What should we do? How in a sermon does a preacher effectively mentor reflective decision-making and set the "what" and "how" of action appropriately in context with "who"? Again, no single sermon can engage all these questions, but over time preaching can show what must be in conversation. A continuing challenge for preaching has to be how to model, and to invite others to join in the conversations—not just about what we should do, but about how we can all be drawn more deeply into life in Christ.

Moral formation has both individual and communal dimensions

Moral decision-making has about it a quality of "the buck stops here." No one else, after all, can make decisions for me. Yet from this it does not follow that I have no moral share in what others do or may have done, even if they are my ancestors. ("My great-grandparents never owned slaves, and I don't use racial slurs" does not mean I have no responsibilities with respect to racism.) The task of preaching is not just to secure the majority vote of an assembly, but to evoke an awareness of community and to energize corporate action. It is easy enough for a preacher to say so. But how does preaching help that actually happen over time?

2. CONDITIONS IN CULTURE THAT RENDER THE PREACHING TASK ESPECIALLY FORMIDABLE

Information overload

Moral decisions are empirically informed decisions: they have to do, as we have said, with "what" and "how" as well as "why." Interpretation, deliberation, significance-weighing cannot take place apart from a feel for the relevant facts. Yet we are constantly bombarded with data from every direction. Information comes, in bits and pieces, from all sides. Cable television with 100 or more stations and computers with all but infinite access to more data overshadow traditional means of news and information from newspapers and radio. The pulpit cannot compete with the sheer volume of mass media. But if there is to be any Christian moral discernment, the pulpit needs to be a place where matters less immediate but more foundational are held up for consideration and assessment. The challenge, for preachers, is not so much a matter of what to say, but how to shape a space within which members of the congregation can deeply listen for that which is of moral significance.

Rush to judgment and the polarization of thought

What makes it so difficult to get a "feel for the facts" is the rush to judgment. Ironically, too much information often leads to the narrowing of focus to one point of view in order to control the data stream. There is no time for assessment and reflection, only reaction. Every matter is politicized by reports of those for and those against. Deliberation and choice are reduced to narrow claims and counterclaims. For example:

• Iraq offered refuge and support to terrorists who sought to attack the United States . . . Iraq had no official contact with the terrorist network of Al Queda and in fact refused any cooperation.

- Stem cell research offers the promise of curing life-threatening injuries and diseases . . . effective stem cell therapies have yet to be developed and will likely be limited in application.

- Human life begins at conception, at which point there is the full genetic make-up of a human person . . . human life begins eight to twelve days after conception when the embryo is formed as cells bonded to form an organism rather than as individual cells that can grow independently from each other.

From stem cell research to gay marriage to the war on terrorism to rebuilding New Orleans, the rush to judgment leaves little room to move between the question of what should be done and questions about what can be done.

We find ourselves caught between increasingly partisan ideological systems that reduce matters to singular ideas or slogans: right to life or right to choose, gay or straight, terrorist or freedom fighter, conservative or liberal. We are called upon to choose sides that are often identified with a particular culture: religious right against liberal left, the developed nations against the undeveloped nations, Christian nations against Islamic terrorists. We are more and more partisan in our considerations and therefore also more and more fragmented apart from any consensus. A lone pulpit voice seems no match for the cacophony that surrounds us. Again, the challenge: how, in the midst of deep divisions, to foster deep listening?

Individual autonomy and the problem of authority

As we are bombarded by information that appears increasingly politicized, claims are challenged, qualified, and often reduced to mere opinion or propaganda. We stop trusting authorities almost altogether. There are no taken-for-granted traditional authorities. The church, science, expert opinion, the press, and the government can't be trusted but must be challenged until—like a jury—each person must make up his or her own mind. This is what is meant by individual autonomy: literally each person gives the law to him- or herself. I decide for myself what to believe and what to do.

Ironically, when people must choose from the cacophony of contested judgments, they may give themselves entirely to one authority. Faith rather than facts. Choices must be made. Some side must be taken: liberal individualism versus conservative dogmatism, secular liberalism versus the religious right, modernism versus traditional orthodoxy. But, whoever has authority—Fox News or the BBC, the political left or the conservative right, Jerry Falwell or Pope Benedict XVI—the individual person has given them that authority. There is no way around the individual. The question is whether I will be informed or not, reactive or not.

In Christian ethics the first claim or principle has been that the individual person must honor his or her conscience. Not to act according to our conscience is to act against our basic values and convictions. If we act against our conscience we act against ourselves. We divide the self. We have false-consciousness. We lose our integrity. The challenge in Christian ethics has, therefore, always been, how do we adequately inform our conscience? For preaching the challenge is, how do we create the space to listen so that it is possible to discern what's happening on a broader, deeper level in terms of God's presence in our lives? Perhaps we might better say that the challenge is to make it possible to create space and offer perspectives in order to hear, question, and assess what is happening around us in order to hear the word of God. For Christians, the challenge of preaching is not only interpreting the world but interpreting Scripture as well.

3. FACTORS IN THE LIFE OF THE CHURCH THAT MAKE IT DIFFICULT TO PREACH SCRIPTURE

Lost biblical and theological literacy

Simply put, more and more of those who claim some sort of Christian identity know less and less of their sacred texts and traditions. "What happens in the book of Genesis after the Fall?" asked a friend and former student of ours who was leading a high school Sunday school class. There was silence, accompanied by blank stares. Finally one of the students raised a hand and tentatively volunteered: "Winter?"

It is less and less possible for preachers to draw upon, refer to, or allude to even the most fundamental pieces of biblical literature, let alone aspects of Christian history or theology. Preachers can "tell the stories," of course, and should. But the problem is, as speakers spend their time and listeners spend their energy "laying again the foundations," as the author of Hebrews chidingly puts it to his congregation,[1] there is less time and energy to engage present moral crises and what they mean for our lives. Telling or retelling the biblical story doesn't in itself enable moral discernment.

Decreased religious community identity

If the previous point can be simply put, so can this one: people don't come to church like they used to! It is not just that fewer people come; those who do come don't show up as often. Too many commitments, too many attractions compete with Sunday worship. "Regular attendance at Sunday worship" (and thus presence for participation in a Sunday sermon) now tends to mean once or twice a month instead of every Sunday. Imagine trying to learn the basics of a language, let alone develop proficiency or creativity, with such limited exposure.

The loss of religious identity is paralleled by an increasing consumer mentality. Those who come to Sunday worship don't check their consumerism at the door. If they don't like what the preacher says, there are all sorts of other church options they can try (if they get around to it).

The loss of religious identity is a challenge for the preacher. But also in play (a factor more healthy but at least as great a challenge) is the increasing diversity of congregations—age, economic status, ethnic background, educational preparation, job description. This can easily mean that those who gather, ostensibly to "be one in the spirit," may for all practical purposes have as many mutually unintelligible frames of reference as the motley group that gathered on the Day of Pentecost. From whence, preachers wonder, will come the Holy Spirit so that persons can hear each other, whatever tongue they may speak?

A restricted focus for the meaning of "narrativity"

"Narrative preaching" has been all the rage among the most recent generation of preachers and homileticians. We have been encouraged to hear and tell "the story of Jesus" and, in turn, encouraged to "find our story in the Bible." That is well and good: it has been needed. The problem with such an approach, if narrowly conceived, is that the Scriptures are turned into something of an Anthology of Sacred Folk Tales (or even Spiritual Aesop's Fables). The Saving Hero (Jesus, a Providential God, or an Outbreaking Holy Spirit) comes to defeat the Villain Satan, rescue us in our sinful predicament, and lead us into life eternal happily ever after.

We intend no disrespect by such a caricature. Scripture *is* about history and salvation. We necessarily speak about salvation history, "those mighty acts by which [God has] given us life and immortality."[2] But reading Scripture solely as salvation history misses other readings and revelations of Scripture. Preachers need to draw upon deeper, richer understandings of what Scripture narrates that will move beyond "what would Jesus do" to the patterns and practices that make possible moral discernment where issues are complex, stakes are high, and perspectives are conflicting.

Alongside the account of God acting in history is the witness of response to the experience of God. Scripture narrates crises and choices. Scripture also witnesses patterns and practices of faith. The challenge for preaching is to have in mind the broader patterns and practices that must be brought into conversation if preaching is to enable moral discernment and formation for the Church.

"Challenge"—over and again that word has punctuated our lean descriptive suggestions as to why moral discernment preaching is so difficult—what preachers are called to confront in such a time as this. We began this chapter by citing a crisis that has become iconic in consciousness—the attacks on 9/11—and another crisis that could still become iconic—Hurricane Katrina. We noted that the understandable response of trauma, the "paroxysm of pain" generated by these crises, has distracted people from the more fundamental and more critical sense of "crisis": "a vitally important or decisive stage in the progress of anything, a turning point" (the definition of the English *OED*, not that of the American *Merriam-Webster Dictionary*). At the end of 2004 there came a "crisis" of exactly the sort the *OED* depicts—one without analogous trauma. Unlike 9/11 and Katrina, nobody could say, "We didn't see it coming." Every four years, in the United States, elections happen. The election of 2004 was, fundamentally, a "crisis"—a turning point. All the factors we have cited in this chapter were in play throughout a campaign that, in the end, the analysts say, turned on "issues of morality."

As preachers and moral decision-makers (and as those whose professions involve systematic reflection on the practices of those disciplines), we are deeply concerned about the processes by which those decisions were made. In the political area, of course, but even more so among those who identify themselves as "church people" or "the faithful." The dynamics of moral deliberation employed, at least on the wider stage of political and religious debate, were severely wanting in terms of careful, thorough, self-reflective discipline. The factors in culture played out with such a frenzy that bitter sloganeering all but took on a life of its own. In our churches, while principles and proof texts were paraded around (or danced around) by preachers and people, it is hard to conclude that the use of Scripture, overall, generated careful discernment or open-minded, open-hearted prayerful attention to the crisis.

What does it mean, under such conditions, to be faithful? What would it mean for preachers to set about faithfully to equip the faithful for deeply faithful—morally responsible—reflection and action? These are not merely rhetorical questions. They draw attention to a pressing need for addressing, from the pulpit, crisis as *turning point*, rather than merely as *paroxysm of pain*.

Listen now, as a preacher in the Church of England (grounding his sermon in the words of Jesus found in Luke 11:42) seeks, quietly but clearly, to foster such a crisis with his congregation regarding how the church confronts questions concerning sexuality.

HAVE WE SOMETHING TO LEARN
FROM THE MILITARY?[3]

"How do People of Faith respond to chronic moral crises of our time: terrorism, economic inequity, ecological mismanagement, disregard for human rights? How do Christian communities address divisive issues that tear at the fabric of their common life?" This is the opening paragraph of the prospectus for a forthcoming seminar on preaching.

The list of chronic moral crises in the first sentence seems not to connect with what is described in the second—"divisive issues that tear at the fabric of their common life." The issue that has torn publicly at the fabric of the common life of the Church of England (and of sister churches of Anglican Communion) has been none of these, but that of homosexuality.

This has rumbled on for years past: it was an issue when I was ordained in the 1980s (when *The Sun* ran the memorable headline "Runcie says: 'Pulpit poofs can stay'"); it flared up about four years ago when Jeffrey John was nominated a bishop; it was the cause of the Windsor Commission seeking ways to keep our different churches in communion; there is talk of setting up parallel provinces so that those (for example in the Nigerian church) for whom homosexuality is simply sinful, do not have to be linked with those (for instance in USA) who have elected homosexual bishops.

I won't go into this at any greater length, but it is clear that the Church of England and her sister churches have been and are torn apart publicly over this issue. One thing that has been very striking to me has been how detached this argument has been from wider society, at least within England. For example, I am part of an independent advisory panel for the Royal School of Artillery at Larkhill, and in that capacity recently observed an exercise a regiment was doing on Salisbury Plain. You may well know that the modern Army has women in equal roles with men, sharing quarters, camps, units; and you may remember too that just a very few years ago—perhaps four—homosexuality in itself ceased to exclude people from soldiering. In the light of the Church's agonies over this, I was amazed at the apparent ease with which the Army has gone from outright exclusion to straightforward acceptance. There were acknowledged to be homosexuals in the units I visited; their presence presented no problems.

Now of course I don't know the extent to which the officers and NCOs to whom I spoke were simply toeing the line; they are all part of an institution that has changed its culture on this during their service, and in which a measure of political correctness is now a requirement. But people I spoke to were adamant that this was not an issue. They said that what mattered was on the one hand trustworthiness—whether a soldier could be relied upon in the extremities where life and death depend upon one's colleagues—and on the other, that the military must reflect the society from which it comes.

The Church may have something to learn here. In the public discussion of issues arising from homosexuality there has been a remarkable degree of judgementalism, and a focus on the particular rather than the ultimately important. In other words, to paraphrase Jesus in today's second reading, we tithe mint and rue and herbs of all kinds, and neglect justice and the love of God.

The whole body of our Lord's reported words is remarkable for the attention that is given to hypocrisy compared with the lack of attention given to sexual matters. I suppose this may be because matters of sex very easily lead us into a focus on the particular (the mint/rue, as it were) rather than the general and important—the love of God and neighbor, the need for integrity and truth.

The Church has given, and continues to give, enormous attention and energy to an essentially inward-looking, and often rather nasty, wrangle about one small element of sexuality. This is convenient, of course, because it distracts us from painful self-questioning about our own sexual morality and motivation, and because by keeping the discussion in-house we can avoid having to face really burning and serious sexual issues. When do you last recall the Church or its leaders in different parts of the world confronting really important matters in which power is being abused? Consider the trafficking of women and children from poverty in eastern Europe and Africa to forced prostitution in countries including our own; the casual cheapening of sexual relations and promiscuity in our culture; the prevalence of sexual tourism; the ease with which society becomes obsessed with paedophilia as uniquely wicked, at the same time as condoning the sexualizing of children's lives and environments.

It is so much cosier, paradoxically, to engage in an internal struggle for the purity of the Church than to help society confront the corruption of the innocent. Would Jesus be saying: woe to you, Anglicans?

Notice what the preacher does, and does not do: rather than telling the congregation how they should think regarding homosexuality, per se, he seeks to redirect and raise consciousness about morally wider and spiritually deeper issues. There is, in fact, a crisis here, he says, one that has been obscured in the protracted and polarizing debates by which the church is allowing itself to be distracted.

What strategies, then, can we preachers develop to help our listeners not only cope with the challenges, but undertake, even welcome, such crises as people of faith? How, in other words, can we systematically and effectively undertake the vocation of preaching toward moral discernment?

Journeys in moral formation are always complex and conflicted—challenging terrain for listeners and preachers alike. For such journeys a map may prove helpful. Maps abstract significant features of a landscape in order to provide direction for would-be-travelers. Here we have formulated seven theses that may serve as a map for our explorations ahead: an approach to Sunday lectionary Scriptures that can deeply engage communities of faith in the dynamics of moral discernment.

Thesis 1: Preaching for moral discernment requires continual interplay between the open-ended narratives of Scripture (where God's actions are proclaimed) and the open-ended narratives of our lives (where God's actions are experienced).

Thesis 2: *Preaching moral discernment requires moving away from focusing narrowly on particular issues or narrowly on the Gospels understood primarily as accounts of "saving history."*

Thesis 3: *Fostering moral discernment and faithful response through preaching also requires moving back and forth between quandaries and practices.*

Thesis 4: *The Christian moral life is centered in six practices: (1) prayer and worship, (2) forgiveness and reconciliation, (3) the formation of households as communities of faith, (4) hospitality as the embrace of the stranger and those in need, (5) citizenship and political responsibility, and (6) reverence for creation.*

Thesis 5: *Preaching for moral discernment needs to undertake directly the adventure it seeks to articulate.*

Thesis 6: *The rhetorical forms of metaphor, narrative, and argument employed in Scripture by "the preachers of the Bible" are the rhetorical forms necessary to effect preaching for moral discernment.*

Thesis 7: *Preaching toward moral formation requires a community of practices that offers its members clear alternatives to those that are prevailing or taken for granted.*

These seven theses point in many directions. The initial theses (1 and 2) focus on the relationship of Scripture and preaching moral discernment. The next two theses (3 and 4) move to our understanding of ethics. Moral discernment is shaped by moral vision as actions are shaped by larger practices. Effective preaching, however, is not given by simply such understandings. Preaching is a matter of communication, a matter of rhetoric (theses 5 and 6). Finally, our identities and actions are made possible by the communities in which we live (thesis 7).

The challenge in preaching as in life is in bringing together what is too easily separated. Tunnel vision and working in silos

besets preachers no less than anyone else. We hope these seven
theses give some sense of what needs to be addressed. We hope to
draw attention to each and to show the relationships between
them. The gap between thought and action, reflection on preaching and the sermon itself, remains. We have, tried, therefore, by
means of selected sermon examples, to evoke a sense of what
preaching to foster moral discernment can sound like.

Notes

1. See Hebrews 6:1–2.
2. Collect at the Liturgy of the Palms on The Sunday of the Passion, *The
   Book of Common Prayer* (New York: Seabury, 1979), 270.
3. This sermon was preached by Edward Probert at Salisbury Cathedral on
   October 1, 2006.

CHAPTER 2

Scripture and Discernment

PREACHING BEGINS WITH A CONVERSATION between Scripture
and the ongoing life of the faith community in the world-at-large.
The word of God is not primarily script on a page but the presence of God in the lives of people, continually calling them to
lives more faithful still. This leads us to our first thesis.

*Thesis 1: Preaching for moral discernment requires continual
interplay between the open-ended narratives of Scripture
(where God's actions are proclaimed), and the open-ended
narratives of our lives (where God's actions are experienced).*

Effective preaching reaches us where we live.[1] Preaching
is not the same as lecturing (either information-dispensing or
admonition-imposing). Preaching is a dramatic verbal event in
which God's judgment and grace immediately engage those who
hear "the word." We authentically preach the word of God
as—and only as—we simultaneously break open the meanings of
Scripture and life so that each resonates with the other.

Preaching is not the bridge between text and context where
exegesis uncovers the truth of a biblical passage that is then
applied to the present context.[2] There is no simple correspondence
between a past text and our present context. Specific readings
from Scripture—from those of ancient Israel to those of newly
founded Christian churches—offer particular, specific texts that

19

witness a people's encounter and response to God in a particular and specific context. These testimonies are set forth in mythic stories, historical narratives, legal texts, poetry and proverbs, prophetic denunciations and annunciations, parables, teachings, and letters. Understanding the context of these writings is why biblical criticism is important to exegesis. But interpreting a text historically in terms of context, audience, and purpose does not itself establish what is to be preached.

Since preaching is the proclamation of the Gospel, our present situation must be interpreted as the occasion of God's presence. Preaching seeks to proclaim God's presence among us—as announcement and invitation, as judgment and grace, as conversion and way of life. Preaching God's presence is a matter of reading both Scripture and our own lives. Interpretation and understanding of past text and present context constitute a circle: each continues to inform the other in what has been called a "hermeneutical circle."[3] A prosaic example may clarify the character of this interpretive circle.

Both of us are gardeners, and both of us have grown roses. Rose gardening can be a challenge but is normally a straight-forward production. Roses are planted in alternating rows. You fertilize, water, and mulch the beds. When humid weather comes, you spray; after the first hard frost, you cut back the canes; in the spring you remove deadwood and begin the cycle again. With a picture of a rose garden in mind, the gardener works accordingly, like a builder with a blueprint.

But both of us undertake perennial gardens as well. No two perennial gardens are alike. A bed of perennial flowers (with an occasional annual in its midst) is not a matter of orderly rows and fixed directions. Perennial gardens involve a succession of blooms from spring bulbs to late summer flowers. Succession, color, mixture, and height all depend on variables that differ from place to place: temperate zone, frost date, soil, water, sun, humidity, plant varieties. Every perennial garden is uniquely challenging. There is no simple picture or singular blueprint; the perennial garden is always in process. Some plants work, some don't. New plants are added, some plants are moved, some plants are taken out altogether. Like preaching, gardening isn't given in a garden book but in the ongoing conversation between received wisdom and gardening itself.[4]

> *Thesis 2: Preaching moral discernment requires moving away from focusing narrowly on particular issues or narrowly on the Gospels understood primarily as accounts of "saving history."*

By themselves, occasional sermons on moral crises *du jour* (or on the importance of moral formation) have little chance of fostering a coherent understanding of Christian faith. Bluntly put, they cannot effectively compete with the media barrage that constantly inundates those who manage, at best, to make it to church an average of twice a month.

But "competition" is not an appropriate preaching strategy anyway; it is intentional, systematic *centering* that we envision. Rather than trying constantly to reach out and snag attention, preaching, we think, should seek to be measured, steady, nourishing; appetite-whetting, reflection-inviting, focus-grounding. In the course of each year, preaching needs to offer a generative account of the practices of the Christian life, not simply in themselves, but as those practices shape and are shaped by decisions we confront. Sermons can't do everything, of course, but sermons can be centering points for hearing the word of God and learning what that means for the life we seek to "live in Christ."

Much of the preaching one hears fails in leading to moral discernment because of a narrow focus on the Gospels to the exclusion of Epistle and Old Testament lessons. Gospel texts seem to lend themselves to neater topics, themes, illustrations, and applications (not to mention shorter sermon preparation time!). "Gospel preaching" also lets preachers think they can hide behind "the words of Jesus," rather than trying to cope with something that sounds complex, offensive, or arcane.

More deeply, however, Gospel-preoccupied preaching is often undergirded by a *de facto* if not explicit assumption of "saving history" (*Heilsgeschichte*), whether evangelical or liberationist.

Such claims of a saving history offer a unified account of Christian faith by reading Scripture as a kind of mystery play in which our life is to be drawn into that of Jesus'.[5] With the birth of Jesus we ask, "Where is Jesus to be found in our lives?" Next we turn to Jesus' life and ministry and ask, "What would Jesus do?" From sayings and parables to Jesus' acts of ministry to miracles to Jesus' death and resurrection, Jesus shows us where to go and how. Instead of revealing the exploration of a way of life, the Bible is the blueprint for our personal salvation history. Preaching in this mode of scriptural understanding becomes a matter of encouraging listeners along a predictable pilgrim pathway rather than of undertaking together the adventure in moral discernment.

Graphically put, we seriously question a deeply engrained notion of sentimental piety: "The Story of Salvation" as it appears in "The Bible"—one that often moves inexorably from "Once Upon a Time," through a single, unambiguous story line to "They All (or at least The Elect) Live Happily Ever After." Not only does such an account present the actions of a Boundless God as a "closed narrative," it also reduces "The Christian Life" to a fixed ideal that is caricatured in images of "the perfect marriage," "the perfect job," "the perfect Christmas"—images that often tragically enslave rather than gracefully liberate and healthily challenge those to whom they are held up.

Instead of seeing Scripture narrowly or only as "saving history," the Bible needs to be read as witness to the different experiences and understandings of God as the community of faith develops over history. Scripture itself is a canon, a collection of writings that develops over time. Texts question and challenge one another just as much as they build one upon another.[6]

- So it is with accounts of creation and the way in which the world is understood. The two creation accounts that begin in Genesis are followed by other accounts, some offering different understandings of creation, others reworking early accounts of creation (see Gen 6:1–4; Ps 74; Job 38–42; John 1, Col 1; Rev 1; and Rev 12:7–13).[7]

• So it is with the understanding of Jesus in the play between the four Gospel texts that begin the New Testament. The play between texts—from the two different accounts of the Beatitudes in Matthew and Luke to the differences in the post-resurrection endings in each of the four Gospels—opens exploration of how different Christian communities understood their faith and sought to be faithful disciples.

Especially important are the Epistle texts appointed for each Sunday in a liturgical year. From the first letter to the Corinthians, addressed to a community threatened by class divisions, to the concern in the First Letter of Peter about how to be a faithful Christian community in an alien and hostile culture, the Epistles take the shape of letters that proclaim Christian faith as they seek to discern what life in God entails. Here are "narratives" every bit as critical to the life of the church as "the stories Jesus told" or the stories that are told about him in the Gospels.[8]

Biblical narratives, in other words, include "narratives of communal discernment" as well as "narratives of salvation history." Through the liturgical year, as explicit or implicit narratives of communal discernment, texts from the Epistles offer the opportunity for the exploration of quandaries and more broadly the practices that shape and deepen the life of faith.

Such explorations in moral discernment will become fragmented unless they are sustained over time. More than the occasional sermon is required. Preaching moral discernment that makes deeper connections about a faithful and holy life requires looking at the lectionary as a whole, from Sunday to Sunday in light of the practices that constitute the Christian life. A particular opportunity is provided in the cycle of readings, and especially the Epistle texts, that fall outside of major feasts in "ordinary time" (the Sundays after the baptism of Jesus on the first Sunday after Epiphany and the Season after Pentecost).

The Sunday lectionary readings, however, are both a blessing and a curse. Following Jewish practice, beginning with the regularized readings of high feast days, lectionaries developed in the early church over the course of the first seven centuries.[9] The blessing is that the lectionary is a means to ensure that the broad witness of the early Christians is heard as a matter of faith in God begun in Israel, culminated in Jesus Christ, and lived out in the earliest communities of Christian faith. Beginning with the proclamation of the biblical texts—engaging laws and stories, songs of praise and lament, prophetic denunciation and annunciation, proverbs and parables, gospels and letters—preaching does not center on the particular vision and judgments of the preacher. The curse of the lectionary is that what was intended as the means of hearing Scripture as a whole can, in fact, narrow preaching to the exposition of biblical texts (most often the Gospels) and fail to address in a timely and ordered way how God is present now and what that means for our present lives.

Thesis 3: Fostering moral discernment and faithful response through preaching also requires moving back and forth between quandaries and practices.

To speak of God present in our lives is to stand in the particular—the moment, the crisis, the issue. The gospel speaks not so much *to* but *through* the concrete choices we confront. God is present here and now, not primarily by way of some overarching monolithic conception of "The Moral Life." Preaching cannot live in abstractions. Preaching requires more than addressing particulars.

The terrorism of 9/11, the cascade of events following Hurricane Katrina, the life and death of Terry Shiavo, the pressure to define marriage in the U.S. Constitution, the debate in European countries regarding standards of dress for Muslim women or the publication of cartoons depicting the prophet Mohammed: these are the crises and quandaries that call for moral discernment. They make us think again and discern what is, for example, the nature of violence and the limits of security, the history and possibilities for a more just society, the purpose of medical treatment, and the nature of marriage. At the same time, we can make sense of how God is present or calling us in crises and quandaries only if we have some larger vision of the Christian life. Specifically, preachers must have in their minds an account of the central practices of the Christian life. By practices we mean the distinctive actions that are central to "life in Christ." Hospitality, justice, worship: such words draw together particular acts as integrally related in realizing some purpose or intention.[10] The act and the purpose, what we should do and why we should do it: this is what the hearer of the Word wants and needs from the preacher.

A crisis in moral decision-making for an individual or a faith community is generated by a genuine quandary: when the behavioral implications of our practices lead in conflicting directions. What does it mean to respond to the homeless with hospitality? Should I directly hand out money to those in need or should I support the shelter and social service ministries? How Christians understand the practices of Christian faith shapes their moral discernment. In this sense, practices are not laws dictating how quandaries are to be resolved. They don't tell us whether we should vote for or against immigration reform, support or oppose increased taxes for education or health. They don't tell us what we should do to protect ourselves against possible terrorists. What an account of Christian practices can do, however, is draw our attention to what is the fundamental character of Christian life and the basic questions Christians need to ask. Practices help us individually and as a community to grasp what is involved in living into Christian faith. Quandaries without practices are unintelligible actions; practices without quandaries are empty abstractions. Preaching that enables moral discernment and formation draws upon the relevance of each for the other.

A Christian account of practices is grounded in Scripture, but never simply given in any specific text. We may speak of practices such as prayer, forgiveness, and hospitality, but what they mean is given only as different scriptural texts are brought together, each addressing a particular moment in the life of the community of faith. For example, hospitality is one way of naming a central practice of the Christian life. Drawing together various scriptural accounts and injunctions, hospitality is an

outward act such as setting aside a tithe to be given to the undocumented alien, the orphan, the widow, and all in need (Deut
14:29). But hospitality is not simply an act of charity; it is also a
relationship of compassion and welcome. The outcast woman at
the well (John 4:7) is acknowledged; she feels heard. In naming
the practice called "hospitality," we draw together, consciously or
unconsciously, actions that seem to belong together, actions that
form a pattern for our lives. An account of practices is not then so
much derived from Scripture as it arises from a conversation
between Scripture and our own experience, and what therein we
regard as the gracious or redeeming presence of God.[11]

It is not enough to have some general sense of Christian
practices. Christians tell the truth, don't worship idols, give to
those in need, read the Bible, and say grace before meals. They
stand for justice, love one another, respect life, and worship
together. Such lists are problematic: they are bits and pieces that
sometimes overlap but are often unconnected. No general list can
express what stands at the center of the Christian life because it
isn't clear how one activity relates to another.[12] Such lists don't
help us connect the particular crises we face to a broader, coherent way of life. Indeed, they may scatter our attention.

The search for the best account of Christian practices is like a
search for a good map. The map must get you from here to there,
but no map shows everything. Some have too much detail; others
fail to show the back roads. Arguments over what map to buy
may be important, but ultimately we judge a map by its usefulness. So an account of Christian practices is to be assessed by its
usefulness in guiding the preacher (and Christian or inquirer in
general) to see what is central to "life in Christ." The difficulty
and danger is that this must be done in a way that avoids gross
generalization ("be loving for God is love") or excessive specifi-
cation ("vote for Proposition 148").

If the map of Christian practices proves too limited, it may be
revised. Some such map, however, is essential for proclaiming and
discerning what the life of Christian faith is all about. Those who
find clear direction by their internal compass are rare. And those
who do, like prophets, tend to follow only particular roads. Amos

speaks to injustice and corruption but offers little to direct our ways into questions of abortion, the continuation or discontinuation of medical treatment, or the stewardship of creation.

Thesis 4: *The Christian moral life is centered in six practices: (1) prayer and worship, (2) forgiveness and reconciliation, (3) the formation of households as communities of faith, (4) hospitality as the embrace of the stranger and those in need, (5) citizenship and political responsibility, and (6) reverence for creation.*

These six practices, we believe, draw together what is central to the Christian life. Christians celebrate their faith in prayer and worship as they form a distinctive community of household. This household is not separate from the world or over-and-against the world but in the world and for the sake of the world. Specifically, the household of faith both discovers and expresses itself in its practice of forgiveness and reconciliation, hospitality to the stranger, citizenship in the world, and reverence for creation. We want to outline the actions that form each of these practices. In this way we may see what needs exploration in order to see what God is calling us to be and to do.

The six practices we propose are "field-encompassing." That is to say, they seek to construe a full sense of the character of the Christian life that Christians share in common. By this we don't mean "the least common denominator" (the minimal upon which Christians could agree). Instead, the six practices identify the character and shape of Christian faith and life as that is witnessed in Scripture and in the ongoing life of the church. The practices make sense of the character of Christian communities, despite disagreement over some basic claims: for example, what poverty means and requires, whether lethal force should ever be used for the protection of innocent life, or whether the purposes of marriage can be realized in same-sex unions. In fact, it is the character of the Christian life that gives rise to such disagreements because certain things matter. The six practices identify and focus attention on the life of Christian faith as a life lived in God as revealed in Jesus Christ as a matter of the ongoing work of the Holy Spirit. They make possible invitation, exploration, and a full proclamation.

Prayer and *worship* are central to the Christian life. Prayer and worship include corporate actions: from the oral reading of Scripture, preaching, and common prayer to sacramental forms of worship such as Baptism and the Eucharist. Prayer itself has a variety of forms: praise and thanksgiving, petition, and confession. Prayer is also meditative: for example, the meditative reading of Scripture or some other devotion text (*lectio divina* or, literally, divine reading). And then there are specific practices of contemplation such as centering prayer. Clustered together as practices of prayer and worship, the particular forms of prayer and worship share common features such as the centering of attention, remembrance, thanksgiving, and beseeching.

Prayer and worship are related to a new life given as a matter of *forgiveness* and *reconciliation*. Such a new life may be variously developed, for example, as law and grace or as bondage and liberation. However understood, the practice of forgiveness and reconciliation draws together those actions by which conversion to new life in God is given.

In turn, life lived in the grace of God is given in daily life beginning with the household, the place where we live and form life together. *Householding* is a broad designation that draws together a range of more particular practices. However preachers might differently develop the particular practices of householding, the importance of the practice is that it draws attention to the basic context of our lives given in meals, companionship, childrearing, education, discipline, entertainment, and work.

Hospitality identifies the actions that welcome the stranger. Beyond responding to the needs of others—to feed the hungry, to care for the sick, to visit those in prison, to work together with those in need—hospitality is to recognize and respect the other as he or she is, as different and unique. The foreigner personifies the stranger, but we are all in some sense strangers to one another, seeking to be known and to be loved. Child and parent, spouse, friend: the practice of hospitality (or lack of hospitality) shapes all our relationships.

Extending beyond household and hospitality, Christians have always struggled to discern the presence of the will of God in the powers and principalities of the world. The practice of *citizenship* draws attention to the range of actions by which Christians have sought to address the needs of others as matters of society: duties to serve and support the political order, and responsibilities for advocacy, prophetic protest, civil disobedience, and even revolution. Here at the center of citizenship are questions of justice.

Finally, Christians' new life in God is a total reorientation or transformation that changes their relationship to creation itself, the natural world and the entire cosmos. Grounded in thanks and praise, creation is seen as God's, as good, and as cause for wonder, praise, and thanks. In the midst of the apocalyptic threat of famine, pestilence, and war to the distinctively modern threat of the destruction of nature, the Christian life assumes a practice of *reverence for creation*.

These six practices serve as lenses for preaching. Our claim is that preachers must look through these lenses in order to keep their attention on what is needed in order to proclaim Christian faith as new life in God. In describing a way of life, the six practices focus questions that Scripture engages, often implicitly rather than explicitly. In turn, practices focus attention on what needs to be explored in order to proclaim that life now.

As the practices of the Christian life must be related one to another, we could begin our account anywhere. But for simplicity's sake we will begin in chapter 3 within the circle of faith by describing more fully the practice of prayer and worship, moving to forgiveness and reconciliation, and then to the household of faith. In chapter 4 we will examine the practices that mark the enlarging circle of faith: hospitality to the stranger, citizenship as a matter of political responsibility, and reverence of creation as our response to nature.

But first, before examining each of these practices in detail, we need to pause long enough to acknowledge the obvious question: "Given what we have said so far, what does preaching for moral discernment look like?" Scripture narratives and life narratives, quandaries and practices—how can preachers interplay all of these in sermons that are narrowly focused neither on an "issue" nor on "salvation history"? How, in other words, can sermons evoke discernment through such dialogue? Here is how a Lutheran preacher tried to explore a current moral quandary in her own community in northern Michigan in a way that, while honoring the biblical context, renders the familiar question Matthew places on the lips of Jesus as anything but piously rhetorical. Her text is Matthew 22:15–22.

IS IT LAWFUL FOR A CHRISTIAN TO GAMBLE?[13]

Jesus walked into the casino at Watersmeet. But in the entrance, with its majestic pillars and domed ceiling, Jesus found himself reminded of that last day he had walked into the temple at Jerusalem.

It wasn't just the pillars at the casino that reminded him of the temple. It was also the hustle and bustle of the people. The temple had never been just a house of worship. It had also been a gathering place, a place where folks met and talked about the issues of their day. Rabbis held forth, and people came to see what was happening, to meet their neighbors, to make the scene.

At Passover, the crowd would become so thick you could hardly move. The temple security would look sharp, and Roman soldiers would even be posted around all the entrances. The uniforms here at the casino looked a little different, but that was about all, as Jesus joined the press of the weekend crowd at Watersmeet.

Delicious smells were coming from the casino restaurant. He'd heard the wild rice soup was out of this world, but it was steak he was smelling. The waitstaff was hard at their work of serving but seemed to be smiling. He'd seen that look before, in the temple courtyard where the animals for sacrifice were bought and sold. People earned a living for their families this way, always grateful for lots of customers.

Nearby the animal stands were the tables where the money changers could be found. They exchanged Roman money—with its idolatrous head of the emperor and inscription declaring the emperor as the son of God—for the temple tokens, house currency. Now, Jesus walked by the casino cashier, where paper money was being exchanged for chips and coin rolls. He saw a woman put on a pair of latex gloves. "The money here is filthy dirty," she explained to Jesus.

Some things seemed different. The sounds were different here at the casino. Instead of people and animals, vendors and rabbis, there was the sound of metal on metal, coins in and coins out, footfalls and voices hushed by carpet, and the faint music of the spinning reels. Small bursts of laughter or cries of excitement occasionally came from the blackjack tables, where the dealers' hands seemed to just float the cards.

The temple columns led not to an altar here, but to a display of a brand-new Dodge Dakota pickup and some shiny new snow-mobiles. "Good luck! You'd look good in one of those snowmo-biles!" someone greeted him, as Jesus stopped to look at these offerings raised up under the dome.

It was there that some people who knew Jesus spotted him. Some looked stunned to see him. "Jesus, should you be in a gambling casino?" they asked. Some turned away guiltily, hoping Jesus hadn't seen them. Others were happy to see him, happy to see Jesus anytime, anywhere. A group—out from work—stopped by to share with him how they had done that night and talk about how the last Sunday's temple talk on steward-ship had gone.

Word spread that Jesus was there in the casino, and now a crowd gathered. "What about it, Jesus?" They put him to the test. "Is it lawful for a Christian to gamble? Is it a sin to go to the casino?"

Jesus had faced this kind of question before. Back in the tem-ple, it had been the Pharisees and the Herodians catching him in the cross fire. The hot issue was whether you can be a good Jew and pay taxes to Rome.

The Herodians were Jews who felt their best interests lay in making friends with the ruling Romans. Look, they argued, the very temple they were standing in was being refurbished beauti-fully by Herod. Why not pay taxes? So what if you did that with coins that had the emperor's head on them? Religion's got nothing to do with it, they argued. Their position was that it was a way to get ahead—an easier living to be had. What does it hurt?

Jesus saw how their way of life, the false rosy outlook, and their brush with power had trapped them. Take care, Jesus thought, to bet the farm that *this* will save you.

The Pharisees, on the other hand, were pretty popular in suggesting that as Jews they shouldn't have to pay the Roman tax on every adult. Who wants to pay taxes, especially to an invading nation, a pagan nation? And, with money that any good Jew would have found filthy to the touch, with that head of Caesar and the inscription proclaiming him a god. Jesus saw the ways that legalism, their tendency to see everything as black and white, good or evil, had entrapped them. Take care, Jesus thought, that your own high standards don't come back to bite you in the butt. Then he asked the closest Pharisee to show him the coin. They all had a laugh as he pulled it out of his back pocket before he could figure out he'd been caught in his own trap.

It was a no-win situation then, and it was shaping up like a trap this time too. Obviously, there were those among them who wanted to hear a strong word from Jesus against gambling and the casinos. Then, there were those who wanted Jesus to say that there was nothing wrong with it. How to answer without getting someone offended? "Come on, Jesus, inquiring minds want to know!" "Yes or no, it couldn't be more simple!"

Jesus thought about what he had seen and heard. The come-ons and the promotions to entice . . . and . . . groups of seniors gathered on a bus to enjoy each other's company, and get out of the house.

He saw people enjoying the soup, an evening out . . . and . . . high rates of interest charged on borrowed money, money people grew desperate for.

He'd seen the vacant, absorbed faces of people as they stared into the colorful machines, mesmerized by the chance of hitting it big, frantically playing as many machines as they could at a time . . . and . . . he'd seen husbands and wives kidding each other over the blackjack table, having fun, and able to walk away.

He'd seen native peoples abandon their heritage . . . and . . . he'd seen the new schools, better housing, more reliable transportation that had benefited the whole tribe.

He'd heard the people who argued that the Indians, sovereign nation or not, should pay taxes on the earnings . . . and . . . the same people, who either didn't know or just didn't think they should report their own winnings to the sovereign IRS on their income tax.

Jesus saw guards, waitresses, cashiers, and hotel clerks who were just happy to have a job to feed their families . . . and . . . Jesus saw people who had lost it all here—homes, families, health, perspective, life savings—lives ruined.

It all took him back to that day in the temple. And it occurred to him that some things never change. Jesus looked at those who were so quick to take what seemed so black and white and clear as the moral high ground for themselves to judge others. He saw how they could be trapped in their own legalism and the self-righteousness that has such a vicious backlash when it turns out that finally the world is a messy, human place. The lines can't be drawn as simply as we thought. Gloves can't just be pulled on to keep us from being involved in the workings of the world.

Then Jesus looked at those who were so quick to embrace the casino scene without reflecting on it, that they were easily trapped by its false and empty promise. Trapped by the neon, the snowmobiles, and the jackpot that is always around the corner, always in the next roll of the dice, the spin of the reel or wheel or deal. Lured by the false hope that this is the way out for the hopeless, or the lonely, or the bored, or the empty—those ripe to be trapped in the greed and the gambling. Feeling this has nothing to do with faith, just play time. Wanting to keep God out of it because to have God in it would make them feel vaguely uncomfortable or ashamed.

No question there is good and evil in this world, thought Jesus. But it's more subtle than we imagine. It's not so simple as just lining faith up on one side and the world on the other and letting them duke it out. We just trap ourselves on one side or another.

There's only one way out of the trap, thought Jesus. We need to draw our lines, our lives, differently. We need to draw not lines of faithfulness and worldliness but lives as a circle. A circle in which our lives come from God and are going toward God. A circle of time over which God is sovereign—Lord of all, Lord always! A circle from which we are called to discern, in any situation, in any realm we find ourselves—in school, work, government, play, even in the casino if we go—how we are honoring God in all things, living our faith, practicing the stewardship of our whole lives.

The question is not if casinos are good or bad, but can those who find gambling dark and evil name God Lord and sovereign even of the casinos? Giving God power and imagination to choose any instrument to work God's will for God's world?

And, can those who gamble at the casinos name God the Lord even of the casinos and the time and the money that they choose to spend there?

Can we all become more whole by taking a moment to bring God into our lives in every situation? Can we set aside our snap judgments and our vague shame, our sense that faith is here and the world is over there, and make a decision instead that names God as the center of our whole lives, as sovereign over the whole world? That acknowledges that there is no corner of our lives or our world that God does not know, does not rule over?

Can they find wholeness, Jesus thought, by giving themselves and their world up to a God who can bring even life and death together, who can make weal and create woe, form light and create darkness, who does all these things like no other can?

So Jesus finally turns to those who are shocked and surprised to find him in the casino—either because they thought he shouldn't be there, or because he found *them* in the casino and they never thought they'd have to meet him there! And while they hold their breaths, waiting for the answer, he asks them a question instead: "Show me the chip used to gamble at the casino. Whose image is stamped on here, and whose title?"

They answer, "The casino logo is on here, and the name of the casino." Then he says to them: "Give therefore to the casino the things that are the casino's."

And then he asks them another question. The one which has the ultimate importance for all of their lives. "And you?" Jesus asks. "Whose image is stamped on you?"

"God's! they say. "We're stamped out in God's image, the image of the God who created light and darkness, the whole world, all that there is, seen and unseen!"

"And whose title do you bear?" Jesus asks.

They say, "Christ's! We were named children of God. We are sealed with the Holy Spirit, marked with the cross of Christ forever, to bear his redeeming word through all the world."

And Jesus says, "Then give to God the things that are God's."

Here the preacher assumes specific Christian practices that shape the sermon in its focus on moral discernment. She also employs specific homiletical principles and sermon strategies in shaping her "message." These will be addressed in the following chapters.

In the context of this chapter on Scripture and discernment, however, it is important to note (and easy to observe) that she seeks to evoke a process of discernment in her listeners rather than to provide a clear and simple Christian moral answer to a very complex social and spiritual issue. And she does so by bringing into conversation the open-ended narratives of Scripture (where God's actions are proclaimed) and the open-ended narratives of our lives (where God's actions are experienced). The effect is to draw our attention to what is the fundamental character of Christian life and the basic questions Christians need to ask.

Notes

1. That is why narrative preaching, the recounting and connecting of stories in Scripture and stories of life, has been so widely embraced as a homiletical theory. See, for example, Fred B. Craddock, *Preaching* (Nashville: Abingdon, 1985); Thomas G. Long, *The Witness of Preaching* (Louisville, KY: Westminster John Knox, 1989); Eugene L. Lowry, *The Sermon: Dancing the Edge of Mystery* (Nashville: Abingdon, 1997);

Jana Childers, *Performing the Word: Preaching as Theatre* (Nashville: Abingdon, 1998).

2. See Edward Farley, *Practicing Gospel* (Louisville, KY: Westminster John Knox, 2003), on "Preaching the Bible and Preaching the Gospel," "Toward a New Paradigm for Preaching," and "Sacred Rhetoric," 71–103.

3. The classic text regarding hermeneutics is Hans-Georg Gadamer, *Truth and Method* (New York: Seabury Press, 1975).

4. By the gardening metaphor—in contrast to Alasdair MacIntrye's view of narrative and daily life in terms of the game of chess in *After Virtue* (Notre Dame: University of Notre Dame Press, 1981) with its ultimate conclusion that brings closure to action—we seek to convey the open-ended character of the canon and the Gospel into which we are called. See Paul Ricoeur's critical assessment of Alasdair MacIntyre in *Oneself as Another* (Chicago: University of Chicago Press, 1992), 157–63.

5. See the critical assessment of such an approach to preaching in Adolf Adam, *The Liturgical Year*, trans. Matthew J. O'Connell (New York: Pueblo, 1981), 19–31.

6. On the relationship of the tension between texts and the unity of Christian witness constituted by the canon of Scripture, see the "debate" between Brevard S. Childs and Walter Brueggemann, e.g., in "Walter Brueggemann's *Theology of the Old Testament: Testimony, Dispute, Advocacy*: A Review by Brevard S. Childs and a Response" in Brueggemann, *The Book that Breathes New Life: Scriptural Authority and Biblical Theology* (Minneapolis: Augsburg Fortress, 2005), 171–79.

7. Gordon Lathrop, *Holy Ground* (Minneapolis: Augsburg Fortress, 2003), 38–45

8. See, for example, F. D. Maurice in *The Kingdom of Christ* (1842): "The deepest writings of the New Testament, instead of being digests of doctrine, are epistles, explaining to those who had been admitted into the Church of Christ their own position, bringing out that side of it which had reference to the circumstances in which they were placed or to their most besetting sins, and showing what life was in consistency, what life at variance, with it"; vol. 1, ed. Alec R. Vidler (London: SCM Press, 1958), 254.

9. See Peter G. Cobb, "The History of the Christian Year," in *The Study of Liturgy*, ed. Cheslyn Jones, Geoffrey Wainwright and Edward Yarnold, 455–71 (New York: SPCK; London: Oxford, 1992). A Common Lectionary is used by most "mainline" Protestant churches. The Common Lectionary differs from earlier Christian lectionaries in that readings from the Old Testament are not chosen thematically in reference to New Testament texts but are chosen so that Old Testament Scriptures are read in sequence from one Sunday to the next. Here references to lectionary readings refer to the Common Lectionary.

10. See Ricoeur, *Oneself as Another*, 152–58.

11. See, for example, Timothy F. Sedgwick, *The Christian Moral Life* (Grand Rapids, MI: Eerdmans, 1999), 150–54.

12. See Dorothy C. Bass, ed., *Practicing our Faith* (San Francisco: Jossey-Bass, 1997). This volume of essays on twelve practices has stimulated a broader discussion of practices of Christian faith but leaves open the question of the relationship of the practices one to another as a matter of Christian faith. See Miroslav Volf and Dorothy C. Bass, eds., *Practicing Theology: Beliefs and Practices in Christian Life* (Grand Rapids, MI: Eerdmans, 2002) for another collection of essays that variously explore what may be the basis in faith for an account of Christian practices.

13. This sermon, preached by Kim Beckmann, appears in her book *Prepare a Road!: Preaching Vocation, Community Voice, Marketplace Vision* (Cambridge, MA: Cowley Publications, 2002), 16–21. It was previously preached at Trinity Lutheran Church in Stambaugh, Michigan, and at Bethany Lutheran Church in Amasa, Michigan.

CHAPTER 3

Prayer, Forgiveness, Householding

In the next two chapters we want to delineate more fully the actions clustered together by each of the six practices we have proposed. Together these offer a vision of the Christian life; individually they shape our attention so that we may address what God is calling us to be and do. Each practice will be understood differently by different persons and traditions. As lenses, however, these differences—for example, between Anabaptist, Roman Catholic, evangelical, feminist, and liberationist—will be family differences. The practices themselves mark the elements that for all are integral to the Christian life.[1]

Our purpose is to offer a sufficiently thick account of each practice so that, despite our differences, it is clear how such an account informs what we see and how we may explore specific quandaries and crises. Such an account of the Christian life, we believe, is necessary if preaching is not to become captive to the particular concerns of the preacher.

PRAYER

In discerning how to respond to immediate quandaries or chronic crises—9/11, the London bombings, hurricanes and tsunamis, the loss of biodiversity, or what to tune into and what to tune out—Christians are called to pray. What should Christians pray for? What is the power of prayer? Questions about the practice of prayer and worship are central to the Christian life and central to moral discernment.

Jesus went into the wilderness and prayed. He honored the Jewish Sabbath as a day set aside from work, a day of prayer and of resting in the Lord. He set forth the Lord's Prayer as a pattern for communion with God. He drew his disciples together for the Passover meal at the end of his life and, as Paul says, called upon them to celebrate his life as the true paschal feast.

The specific actions and understandings of prayer and worship are varied, but at the heart of prayer and worship are remembrance, praise, and thanksgiving.[2] We give thanks to God for all that is, not only for our lives but for creation itself. "In the beginning when God created the heavens and the earth . . . God saw that it was good" (Gen 1:1, 25). It is out of remembrance and thanks for what life is meant to be that we praise God and beseech God to be with us, to heal and to make whole.

Whether intercessory prayer is a call for divine intervention or a matter of commending ourselves to God in the midst of whatever happens ("thy will be done"), intercessory prayer is the other side of thanksgiving.[3] From the depths of prayer we are aware of the distance or disparity between the good that has been given and the reality of our lives. This leads to prayers of examination, confession and repentance. Attention is drawn to the fault lines that have been opened between God and ourselves until we turn to God in mercy and know that we are not our own but live only by grace. Moreover, we are called to pray together. Our thanks and praise and our prayers for ourselves and for the world are sustained and enlarged in corporate prayer—by its shape or form, by the voices of those about us, and by their loving presence.

Individual and corporate prayer and worship are variously understood. This is reflected in the many different kinds of prayer and worship: Ignation exercises, Celtic prayer, prayer chains, *lectio divina* and other devotional reading, centering exercises, meditation on icons, *ars moriendi* (the arts of dying), retreats, journaling, pilgrimages, walking the labyrinth, prayer and praise, daily offices, and Eucharist/Holy Communion. While

thanksgiving and beseeching run through all such forms of prayer
and worship, they all focus our attention. As spiritual masters
from across religious traditions have said, the first and fundamental principle of prayer is "be attentive."[4]

Prayer may be focused with or without images, whether
through the image of the Word or of an icon or by withdrawing
from images altogether. As a matter of contemplation or what is
called *catophatic* prayer (literally, prayer with images), praying in
images or through stories draws our attention to the way God
has been and is present in our lives and in the lives of those about
us. Praying without images is a kind of pure or empty meditation. Called *apophatic* prayer (literally, prayer without images),
attention is withdrawn from the train of thought attached to particular objects of the world and to the objects of memory so that
we are given to the immediate present and the sheer presence of
God that surrounds us. For both catophatic and apophatic
prayer, prayer is a kind of awakening, a quieting of the soul, and
a preparation for listening to new voices that may speak of the
presence and call of God in our lives.

The character of corporate worship is likewise variously
interpreted, but what is central to these interpretations is captured by the word *liturgy*. Whether formal or informal, highly
scripted or more extemporaneous, corporate worship is liturgical
in the original meaning of the word liturgy. *Liturgy* means "the
work of the people." In worshiping together individual prayer is
broadened and supported. As in the case of Baptism and Holy
Communion/Eucharist, the gathered community of faith enacts
the faith so that what is said is lived: for example, in forgiveness,
acceptance, and communion.

However fully developed and more specifically understood,
the practices of prayer and worship are central to Christian
formation and to hearing how God is present and calling us now
in the crises of our lives. These practices should not be assumed
in preaching. Instead, preaching that addresses particular events
must continually address the central place of prayer.

Rowan Williams, Archbishop of Canterbury, offers one
account of how prayer and worship are integral, essential, to any

Christian response to moral quandaries and crises. In *Writings in the Dust* he describes his own experience at Trinity Church, Wall Street, in New York City immediately following the terrorist attacks of 9/11. In a series of meditations, Williams follows the itinerary, the journey, of moral discernment. He begins with breathing. When he escaped from the buildings at Trinity Parish just a few blocks from the Twin Towers, it was hard to breathe. The air was thick; smoke and dust were pervasive. Space was emptied of city life. The danger, though, was filling the void too quickly, "when what we need is to learn how to live in the presence of the void."[5]

In the midst of violence where our lives are threatened, we initially react. Since we cannot take flight, we fight. Our immediate response is to identify and destroy the enemy. We seek a scapegoat. The terrorist is evil; we must search and destroy all "would-be-terrorists." So "the war" on terrorism is born. Or we react by identifying the evil as our unilateral response to terror: the terrorist is not evil but only reacting to oppression; the colonial power becomes the scapegoat. Either response is reactive.

As Williams emphasizes, what we first need in times of crises is silence: silence to feel our loss and to mourn, silence to listen beyond our own immediate reactions; silence to pray and to feel God's presence and grace before and beyond our own judgments. Prayer quiets us and opens us to discern what is happening, how God is present, and what that means for our lives. In prayer we remain with the events that overwhelm us; we remember what has happened; we pierce the clouds of rubble and dust that have descended from the sky; we see the victims; we feel our cry of shock and horror.

In invocation and lament—nothing more and nothing less— we acknowledge the holy ground where we stand. Here we cannot grasp God and secure ourselves from our terror and grief by some immediate plan of action. Rather, in prayer—over days and weeks, even years—our first reaction of fight or flight is stopped, and we are returned to the scene of action and to our full array of emotions. In this prayer there is a purging of ourselves.

Traditionally Christians speak of purgation as a kind of cleansing, clearing, chastening. In this space, opened through our purgation, we can listen to our emotions and to the longing of our heart. But more, quieted, non-reactive, we can hear the voices that were before only threatening or overwhelming. For example, those who mourn voice the horror of destruction, the possibilities and limits of consolation, and the obligation to provide basic safety. Terrorists in turn become persons through whom we may hear the frustrations, anger, and longings of a world greater than "our own."

Prayer is, moreover, more than individual. We come together as a community of care and embrace to pray, to listen to Scripture, and to celebrate our faith in God. As a community of faith we are carried along, comforted in our shock and sorrow and held so that we know that we are not alone. Gathered together in offering ourselves to God in Holy Communion/Eucharist, we claim and experience in our brokenness, in bread broken and wine poured out, the reality of our life in God as death and new life. Here the community of faith knows a truth that "passes understanding." We hear not only through Word but in the life and sacrament of the Church. And together these form our discernment of what is happening and what we are called to be and to do.

This sketch of prayer and worship maps the character of prayer and worship as they may shape our responses to quandaries and crises. Metaphorically put, these practices are akin to the riggings for sails, raised by the preacher, waiting to be filled by the Holy Spirit. The riggings don't determine how the wind will blow, and what course will be set. But without the riggings—without attention to the practices of prayer and worship—we are unable to discern the course we should take.

The biblical readings for the first Sunday in Advent, for example, are not about prayer and worship but about the kingdom of God. The day of the Lord is a day of judgment. The judgment is against those who have turned from God and failed to become a holy people. Jesus brings forth this day and calls us to awaken to what is happening, to "be ready, for the Son of Man is coming at an unexpected hour" (Matt 24:44).

The Advent readings invite the preacher to speak to a central claim of Christian faith: Christian faith is a new way of life distinct from the prevailing culture. Terrorist attacks, hurricane relief, the homeless and working poor, the devastation of AIDS in the two-thirds world, withdrawal from the world's woes into self-indulgence marked by Christmas gift-giving: the crises of the moment are matters of judgment against our divided world and our failure to become a holy people. The good news is that judgment is promise because it presents us now with a choice of how we will respond.

But all depends on awakening from our sleep. Here, then, prayer and worship come to the fore to focus our attention so that we may discern what is happening in the world about us and what is happening to ourselves. We can then feel and hear God's deepest desire that we be reconciled, be at one, at peace, with ourselves and with the whole world. Prayer and worship are offered in response to God, as thanksgiving and beseeching but first of all as a matter of awakening ourselves to God. They should bring us to our senses as they enable us to listen to God's judgment and call.

FORGIVENESS AND RECONCILIATION

The practice of forgiveness and reconciliation stands at the heart of Christian conversion into a new life. It focuses attention on the "human problem" and the Christian response. Preaching that seeks to enable moral discernment is necessarily shaped by understandings of forgiveness and reconciliation.

The human problem of sin is moral as well as religious. Morally we want to succeed, to choose rightly, to avoid failure. When failure comes—like a marriage ending in divorce—we feel that we are failures, our relationships are broken, and there is no hope in us.[6] To hope again we must be released from our failures, our relations must be renewed, and our trust restored. There must be forgiveness of sins and reconciliation of relationships.

For the individual to forgive, to embrace those who have done us harm, is to acknowledge them as brothers and sisters and to let go of resentment and the desire for revenge. To forgive is not, however, simply a moral act, something that we can do for ourselves. We can forgive only when we acknowledge that we too are broken and separated in sin. This is why John the Baptist calls for the repentance of sin and Jesus teaches us to pray, "Forgive us our sins, for we ourselves forgive everyone indebted to us" (Matt 6:12; Luke 11:4). In order to forgive and be reconciled, our attitudes of righteousness and self-sufficiency must be changed. Our change must be of the heart, which is something we cannot effect ourselves. So Christians speak of amazing grace that comes from being loved, forgiven, accepted, embraced.

Christians have explored forgiveness and reconciliation under various theological headings: for example, justification, new birth, sanctification, and liberation. In terms of actions, Christians have specified particular actions that seek to open up the individual person to God's grace and to draw him or her into that world of grace. Central to these actions is repentance, called for in Scripture and developed in the church as a matter of the examination of conscience and the confession of sin.[7]

In the first centuries of the church, confession of sin was once-and-for-all as part of the preparation for initiation and baptism into the Christian faith as a distinct and different way of life. However, as the baptized fell back into sin and were separated from the community of faith, confession of sin became an ongoing practice. The understanding of how such examination and confession effects conversion to new life is expressed in Augustine's *Confessions*.

For Augustine, confession was not narrowly a matter of listing sinful actions. Instead, the act of confession was the occasion to reflect on why we did what we did. The purpose of confession is to examine our desires, what we thought we desired and what are our true desires. As he recalls in his *Confessions*, the stolen pear gives no lasting delight.[8] To examine and feel again the difference between immediate desires and lasting desires is to open ourselves to the love of God, the end of all our desires.

The examination of conscience has been variously developed in particular Christian communities. For example, forms of examination have ranged from primary reflection on the Ten Commandments to a focus on the seven deadly sins, from preparation for sacramental confession to devotional readings (such as John Bunyan's *Pilgrim's Progress*), from forms of journaling to spiritual direction. Altogether, the purpose remains the same: to identify false desires in order to effect repentance, sorrow, and contrition, which open the self to grace by which love is transformed from oneself to others.[9] Grace happens in this turning from self to other. This reflects Augustine's own basic theological conviction: sin is the contraction of the human spirit in turning in upon itself; grace is the expansion of the human spirit in the love of others.[10]

This moment of conversion necessarily leads to restitution. To be truly sorry that you stole your neighbor's land means that you must be willing to return the stolen property. This is why the developing law from ancient Israel through Jewish Talmudic law details what is owed or due given our sins against one another. Hence the practice of forgiveness and reconciliation can never be separated from justice.

Forgiveness, however, remains a gift, especially evident when nothing can be done to restore the wrongdoing, for example, in cases of death or bodily injury. This is what makes forgiveness and reconciliation so radical—foundational to Christian faith itself. Reconciliation is never simply a matter of restitution. This is witnessed most powerfully by the persons and communities that claim the other regardless: the welcome by the father of the prodigal son, the claim of nonviolence and the refusal to take the life of the very person who would harm us, the care that abides by those in need whatever the cost.

Rape, divorce, racism, and other forms of discrimination, war and opposition to war, or simply the everyday injuries in a competitive world: these reflect and cause the deep fissures in our lives. As a matter of proclaiming God's grace and reconciliation, preaching should address these lines that divide and separate us. This requires addressing the dynamics of sin given as resentment and anger, guilt and the sense of inadequacy or unworthiness, anomie or alienation, separation and solitude. Such explanations of the dynamics of sin are a matter of moral discernment, a matter of exploring how we live in relationships beyond resentment and separation, how we love, how we bear witness to God's call, and how we become advocates of God's justice.

The voice of God, though, is never general. This means preaching where forgiveness and reconciliation are needed, in the midst of the crises and quandaries of our lives. What, for example, does forgiveness and reconciliation mean and require after the violence of 9/11, the London subway bombings, or the deep social divides revealed by natural catastrophes? And how does forgiveness and reconciliation begin in our relationships in our families and among friends? Such preaching then reaches beyond the individual to corporate reflections on what it means to be the body of Christ as the witness or sacrament of God's reconciliation of the world.

The problem central to all such explorations of forgiveness and reconciliation is the problem of memory.[11] We cannot forgive what we don't remember. In our own lives we cannot be reconciled to that which remains repressed or hidden. For example, childhood abuse gives rise to anger and lack of trust, which results in diffidence and the lack of vulnerability in relationships. The sins of the fathers and mothers set the children's teeth on edge (Exod 34:7; Jer 31:29; Ezek 18:2)—and they then reenact the sins of the parents. Until the source of our brokenness is named and addressed, there can be no reconciliation. So it is also with human communities. Violence against native peoples, immigrants, women and children, the innocent killed in the name of war: until the fractured lives of all are remembered and addressed, the human community remains broken.

If preaching is to enable moral discernment, it must recall and revisit our past and explore what has been lost or forgotten and why "what is remembered" is remembered as it is. This opens new ways of morally discerning what we are called to do. South Africa's Truth and Reconciliation Commission led by Desmond Tutu is the most well-known example of such public confession that begins a process of reconciliation and the new birth of a nation.[12] What, the preacher might ask, needs to be remembered in order to understand and live beyond the anger and antagonism opened by 9/11, by Hurricane Katrina, by immigration legislation, or by gay marriage and marriage amendments? Here again, as with the practice of prayer and worship, the practice of forgiveness and reconciliation do not set an agenda or program for preaching. Rather, it makes clear what needs to be addressed in the crises and quandaries of our life if the Gospel is to offer new life.

HOUSEHOLDING

The third practice within the circle of Christian faith is what we call householding. There can be no new life apart from forming a household, a place to live that connects us in the world and to the world. Householding focuses our attention on how we live and shape our daily life so as to live more deeply in relation to God. In this sense, householding draws together a range of more particular actions that may themselves constitute distinct practices.

The household is a little economy. In traditional society the household produced, bought, and sold in order to procure the basics for life and for its own livelihood. It was also the place of family nurture and formation given in the social interactions of daily life, for example, in such basic activities as storytelling, meals, daily rituals, play, entertainment, work, child rearing, education and training, and economic exchange. As such, all householding is a matter of asceticism, literally a matter of discipline in order to reorient and train our desires. Finally, the household was the threshold to the larger world, the place of interactions that formed the individual—as a matter of skills, expectations, and duties—as a member of the larger community. The meaning of the household can only then be understood when the household is paired together with the public. The household is not private, a haven from the world. The household is what establishes the bonds of community that form a people as a whole.[13]

This understanding of the household is reflected etymologically. In German the word *Haus* has meant the place that holds our possessions. In Greek the house (*ekios*) was understood as an economy, a place of exchange, a place of interaction, not only between members of the household but between the household and the world-at-large. This is reflected in the close association of the two Greek words forming the English word *economy*, house (*eikos*) and order (*nomos*); hence, an economy is the order of the household.

The practice of householding should raise in our minds specific quandaries about the decisions we make that form our daily lives. For example, Christian households seek to honor the sanctity of life. What then does this mean in the care of persons who may be dying or suffering from an incurable disease or injury? When is "enough" enough?[14] More broadly, what does care require in order to raise or embrace a child or adult in the human family? What must we do so that no child is left behind? Or in matters of human sexual relationships, what may be most significant are questions about our deepest desires—how desire may be formed or distorted in and out of marriage, for singles, in celibacy, for homosexual persons as well as for heterosexual persons, from adolescence to older age.[15]

In matters of reproductive choices, a great array of quandaries is posed. Should a couple who are carriers of genetic traits that may be debilitative or deadly, such as cystic fibrosis, conceive a child and accept whatever child is born? Or should they abort a fetus who is diagnosed with cystic fibrosis? Or should they conceive a child through *in vitro* fertilization by a donor in order not to bear a child with cystic fibrosis? Or should they use *in vitro* fertilization themselves and then pre-implantation genetic diagnosis (PGD) in order to identify an embryo to implant that does not have cystic fibrosis? Or should they adopt a child? Or should they choose not to have children? Beyond answers, such varied decisions raise the question, "what are families for?" What then is the meaning of children and what is it to welcome children into our lives?[16]

Perhaps most fundamentally, the practice of householding raises questions about what has traditionally been termed *asceticism*. What disciplines should govern the household? What is not to be done or limited, most notably patterns of purchase and consumption, including the visual and the vocal? When should we be "plugged-in" and when should we "pull the plug"? Positively, what practices should be central to our daily lives? How should we spend our time together? How do we dwell together? This is the age-old quandary of what it is to be in the world but not of the world, to love the world as God's creation but not to love the world excessively.[17]

The importance of conceiving of the Christian life in terms of the practice of householding is that householding raises attention to specific quandaries but more broadly than when quandaries are addressed only in terms of moral principles. Householding places such quandaries in the fuller context of what it means to be family where life is given in relationship to God.

And once again, developing an understanding of the Christian household does not resolve quandaries or crises. It focuses attention. Householding is a reminder that life is given through a set of actions that open and sustain what is the divine economy. Here is a counter to the contemporary ethic of individualistic self-fulfillment.[18] As with Adam and Eve, the "other" is a gift to us. Spouses and children evidence this most clearly. Others call us out of ourselves—not narrowly as a matter of care but also as a matter of delight. We are befriended as we offer ourselves up in the care of each other. As Jesus says, "No one has greater love than this, to lay down one's life for one's friends" (John 15:13). "I do not call you servants . . . but I have called you friends" (John 15:15).

The practice of Christian householding may, in fact, be the root metaphor for speaking of the Christian life. The church is, after all, "the household of God" (1 Tim 3:15), not as a separate household but as the gathering together of particular households in common practice and life signed and celebrated most fully in Eucharist/Holy Communion.[19] For the preacher, the Gospels call us into this life while the Old Testament lessons and the New Testament Epistles offer the broader witnesses of communities of faith struggling to form the people of God. The Epistles particularly evidence the distinctive way of life that Christians sought in response to Christ. They bear witness to Christ as they seek to form the household of faith. As Augustine later said of the church, "You are the body of Christ, in you and through you the work of the incarnation goes forward."[20]

Notes

1. As Alasdair MacIntyre has argued, what constitutes the identity of a tradition is not agreement on all matters or on a shared set of claims but a shared agreement on what matters about which persons then disagree and argue as they seek to refine or develop their understandings. As he says, "A living tradition then is an historically extended, socially embodied argument, and an argument precisely in part about the goods which constitute that tradition" (*After Virtue*, 222).

2. For an overview of understandings of worship and prayer, see Susan J. White, "Worship," and David Scott, "Prayer," in *Christianity: The Complete Guide*, ed. John Bowden (London: Continuum, 2005), 1250–52, 964–73; more broadly, see Philip Zaleski and Carol Zaleski, *Prayer: A History* (Boston: Houghton Mifflin, 2005).

3. See Gordon Lathrop, *Holy Things: A Liturgical Theology* (Minneapolis: Fortress, 1993), 55–59.

4. See Pierre Hadot, *Philosophy as a Way of Life*, trans. Michael Chase (Oxford: Blackwell, 1995), 81–144.

5. Rowan Williams, *Writing in the Dust* (Grand Rapids, MI: Eerdmans, 2002), 10.

6. See, for example, what the French philosopher Jean Nabert calls failure, solitude, and fault (as in the geological faults that open chasms that threaten to destroy us) and Paul Ricoeur has biblically described as sins (acts), sin (relations), and defilement. See Jean Nabert, *Elements for an Ethic*, trans. William Petrek, (Evanston, IL: Northwestern University Press, 1969); Paul Ricoeur, *Symbolism of Evil*, trans. Emerson Buchanan (Boston: Beacon Press, 1967), 25–157; and Edward Farley, *Good and Evil: Interpreting a Human Condition* (Minneapolis: Fortress, 1990).

7. See Bernard Poschmann, *Penance and the Anointing of the Sick*, trans. Francis Courtney (New York: Herder & Herder, 1964).

8. Augustine, *Confessions*, trans. Henry Chadwick (Oxford: Oxford University Press, 1991), Bk. II.iv–x (9–18), pp. 28–34.

9. See Michael Foucault, "Technologies of the Self," in *Technologies of the Self*, eds. Luther H. Martin, Huck Gutman, and Patrick H. Hutton, 16–63 (Amherst, MA: University of Massachusetts Press, 1988); and Albrecht Diehle, *The Theory of the Will in Classical Antiquity* (Berkeley: University of California Press, 1982), 123–44.

10. Augustine, *The City of God*, Bk. XIV, edited by R. W. Dyson (Cambridge: Cambridge University Press, 1998), chapters 13, 14.

11. See H. Richard Niebuhr, *The Meaning of Revelation* (New York: MacMillan, 1941), esp.80–87. As Niebuhr says, "To remember all that is in our past and so in our present is to achieve unity of self. . . . That such conversion is not easily completed but rather a permanent revolutionary movement is evident. It must go on throughout the whole of a life-time because the past is infinite and because sin enters anew" (86).

For a recent analysis of this problem, see Paul Ricoeur, *Memory, History, Forgetting* (Chicago: University of Chicago Press, 2005).

12. Demond Tutu, *No Future without Forgiveness* (New York: Doubleday, 1999).

13. On the recent focus of historical studies of the family in late antiquity and early Christianity, see *Families in the New Testament World: Households and House Churches*, eds. Carolyn Osiek and David L. Balch (Louisville, KY: Westminster John Knox 1997); and Joseph H. Hellerman, *The Ancient Church as Family* (Minneapolis: Fortress, 2001).

14. For a review of theological perspectives on medical care and honoring the sanctity of human life, see Stephen E. Lammers and Allen Verhey, eds., *On Moral Medicine*, 2nd ed. (Grand Rapids, MI: Eerdmans, 1998), esp. 193–266, 639–78.

15. Reviewing the current discussions of human sexuality as a matter of households, see Don S. Browning et al., *From Culture Wars to Common Ground: Religion and the American Family Debate*, 2nd ed. (Louisville, KY: Westminster John Knox, 2000). For a historical account of the changes in marriage from primarily a social, economic, and political institution to a relationship of love between two persons, see Stephanie Coontz, *Marriage: A History* (New York: Viking, 2005). For a review and assessment of the current discussion, see Margaret A. Farley, *Just Love: A Framework for Christian Sexual Ethics* (New York: Continuum, 2006).

16. See David H. Smith and Cynthia B. Cohen, eds., *A Christian Response to the New Genetics* (Lanham, MD: Rowman & Littlefield, 2003).

17. See, for example, Catherine M. Wallace, *Selling Ourselves Short* (Grand Rapids, MI: Brazos, 2003); William Schweiker and Charles Mathewes, eds., *Having: Property and Possession in Religious and Social Life* (Grand Rapids, MI: Eerdmans, 2004); and Maria Antonaccio, "Asceticism and the Ethics of Consumption," *Journal of the Society of Christian Ethics* 26 (Spring/Summer 2006): 1:79–96.

18. For the most sustained critique in contemporary Christian ethics, see Stanley Hauerwas, for example, *The Hauerwas Reader*, eds. John Berkman and Michael Cartwright (Durham, NC: Duke University Press, 2001), 539–622.

19. See, for example, Lisa Sowle Cahill, *Family: A Christian Social Perspective* (Minneapolis: Fortress, 2000).

20. This quote variously attributed to Augustine appears to be a paraphrase of his Eucharistic theology expressed in Sermon 272. See *The Works of Saint Augustine: A Translation for the 21st Century*, ed. John E. Rotelle, O.S.A., trans. Edmund Hill, O.P. (New Rochelle, NY: New City Press, 1993), III/7, 300–301.

CHAPTER 4

Hospitality, Citizenship, Reverence for Creation

As WE HAVE DESCRIBED in the last chapter, prayer and worship, forgiveness and reconciliation, and householding focus on life within the body of faith. These three practices, though, already include the fact that the Christian life is always lived in response to the world. We conceive of the Christian response to the world as three-fold: hospitality as response to the stranger, citizenship as the political response to the principalities and powers that structure our world, and reverence for creation as a response to the goodness of nature. As before, practices draw together more specific actions in terms of basic purposes and intentions. As such, they don't determine what to do or what to preach, but they open the door to what must be addressed and explored if preaching is to give word to an incarnate Christian faith.

HOSPITALITY

The stranger stands at the heart of Christianity. The faith of Israel is born in response to the stranger. Beginning with Abraham, Isaac, and Jacob as wandering Arameans, the Israelites began as nomads where hospitality was an absolute demand. In arid lands you are able to carry at most only a few days of food and water. There is no surplus, stored and ready for the time of need. You are naked in the land. And so you must live with open hands, receive what is given from the land and from those you meet. In such a society, you must welcome the stranger who is in need for you also will be a stranger in need. So the nomadic code is strict about guests: they are to be welcomed, offered food, water, a place to sleep, and some provisions before they continue on their way.

The radical hospitality of nomads recognizes the absolute dependence that one nomadic group or person has on another. When the Israelites crossed over the river of Jordan and settled in the land of Canaan, they continued to enjoin such hospitality. As recorded in the law of Moses, "The LORD your God is God of gods and Lord of lords, the great God, mighty and awesome, who is not partial and takes no bribe, who executes justice for the orphan and the widow, and who loves the strangers, providing them food and clothing. [Hence,] you shall also love the stranger, for you were strangers in the land of Egypt" (Deut 10:17–19).

With the settlement of Canaan, Israel develops as an agrarian and commercial society. Food is grown and stored. Labor is specialized. Goods are traded within the land of Israel and with those living in the surrounding Mediterranean basin. A king rules. A military is raised. There is hope for security and prosperity in contrast to the insecurity and stark reality of nomadic life. The danger of such societies is identifying the meaning of their lives with security and prosperity at the expense of hospitality to the stranger.

For the Israelites, however, the originating vision of hospitality continues. The claims of hospitality are, for example, given in the call for Jubilee. Recalling the tradition of ancient Israel as expressed in the Covenant Code (Exod 21:2–6 and 23:9–11), the first text from the law code in Leviticus (25:8–12) refers to the fiftieth year in the land as Jubilee. Following seven times seven years, Jubilee is the Sabbath of Sabbaths. As Moses speaks from Mount Sinai: "You shall have the trumpet sounded aloud; on the tenth day of the seventh month—on the Day of Atonement—you shall have the trumpet sounded throughout all your land. And you shall hallow the fiftieth year and you shall proclaim liberty throughout the land to all its inhabitants." (Lev 25:9–10)

As the Sabbath of Sabbaths, Jubilee is a time of rest, a time to give thanks, and the time to live as we were created to live, not in domination but in sharing together as stewards in God's world. Jubilee is then the time of the full restoration of the land and people. Specifically, Jubilee is the year when throughout the land of ancient Israel, the fields are to be left uncultivated, slaves are set free, lands and houses in the open country that had been held in debt are given back to their owners.[1] As in the Exodus, this freedom, this deliverance, is a matter of hospitality. Jubilee ensured that those indentured as slaves were able to return as full members of the community by restoring to them the land they had sold and lost.

The originating vision of hospitality is likewise pressed to the center of the proclamation of faith in God in the prophetic tradition with its singular emphasis on God's justice: recognizing and meeting the needs of the stranger regardless of the consequences. For Christians, Jesus intensifies and fulfills this revelation. God is fully present in our life as we are called to embrace the poor, the stranger, and all those in need. In the Gospel of Matthew, after identifying those who are strangers—outsiders, those without property, with no standing as citizens, those who are hungry, thirsty, naked, sick, and in prison—Jesus identifies himself (and thus God) with the stranger. Only in receiving and caring for them do we receive God himself. In this embrace is eternal life (Matt 25:31–46).

What Jesus teaches he lives. He shares table fellowship with the poor, women, the outcast, the stranger. This is the life that the hymn in Philippians (2:5–11) speaks of as *kenosis*, a life of self-offering that concludes in the Last Supper, the cross, and resurrection. This is Jubilee, the eschatological kingdom of God, a kingdom that is already present even as it is beyond us in the stranger who calls us into the future.

As all parents know with their children, even those closest to us are strangers. No one mirrors our selves. Other persons call us to recognize them in their difference and so to care for them as distinct individuals with particular needs and longings. More than teach us, they call us to love in a world that is not our own. Instead of turning to hold fast to our private world, in the love of the stranger we are stretched out of ourselves into creation. We therefore say that we meet God in the face of the stranger.[2]

As hospitality begins with the recognition of the other as a person, it entails the specific moral claim that we share a common humanity. So Jews and Christians confess that we are made in the image of God and all are members of the human family. This claim sees in the Genesis story of Adam and Eve that we are sons and daughters born from a single line of parenthood, despite being scattered over the earth, often at odds and unable to understand each other because of the many different languages we speak. Our life is not independent but given in a larger economy, in an exchange of the gift-giving of oneself with another: mother and child, teacher and student, neighbors and friends, strangers and those in need. In the embrace of the stranger, we enter into what Christians call the divine economy or the household of God. As the Letter to the Hebrews says, "Do not neglect to show hospitality to strangers, for by doing that some have entertained angels [who are the messengers of God] without knowing it" (Heb 13:2).

As a practice, hospitality draws our attention to what is central to Christian faith and to what that means for our daily life. As a matter of intent, hospitality is marked by respect, concern, and care for the other that they may share fully in the divine economy. As a matter of action, hospitality begins in meeting immediate needs—food, clothing, shelter—and extends to provide the support necessary to live a life that sustains individuals and families that they may live with self-respect as participants in the broader household that ultimately embraces all people.

What hospitality requires is not then simple, as if a singular action was all that was needed. Meeting immediate needs in a time of crisis is one thing, especially when those needs are specific and limited. To recognize the elderly and infirm and to open a door or help them up or down a flight of stairs is a simple matter. To offer continuing care and support is quite another matter. The larger horizon of possible actions opened by hospitality is brought into focus through the more particular questions of justice and what may be called the practice of citizenship.

CITIZENSHIP

In terms of hospitality, in an agrarian society—to say nothing yet of an industrial society or a post-industrial society—the absolute ethic of giving is no longer a necessity but an impossibility. To plant requires seeds. These must be stored for spring planting. They cannot all be given away: if you do, you will be unable to provide both for yourself and for many others besides.

So, for example, the famine in Somalia in the early 1990s worsened as seed was taken and eaten so that there was little seed to plant. Farmers then left the land. Refugee centers, already burdened, were overwhelmed. Food was then given by other countries. As it was distributed, the price of crops from local farmers plummeted and they too were forced from their land into refugee centers. A dire plight became desperate, and all the more so as armed gangs terrorized the people and stole the food and supplies that were given. The absolute nomadic ethic fails in other contexts. To give all without reserve or condition to those in need will in many contexts actually fail to meet those needs.

Morally, the absolute demand for hospitality leaves us with the classical moral conflict between an ethic of duty and an ethic of consequences. We are obliged to welcome and care for those in need, but an immediate response to a particular individual may conflict with realizing the broader goal of creating the conditions where need is met for not only the one but the many. This is the question of justice, especially the question of distributive justice. How do we fairly distribute goods and services, opportunities and burdens, given the absolute worth of every individual person?[3]

Questions of distributive justice are fundamentally questions of citizenship. The citizen is a member of a city or society. As citizens we are not bound only one to another, individual to individual. Rather, as citizens we are responsible to the body politic, for the commonwealth, for the well-being of the whole. Specifically for Christians, the practice of citizenship stands as the counterpoint to the practice of hospitality. The demands of hospitality are absolute. The demands of citizenship are consequential.

War, famine, and plagues, terrorism and natural disaster— 9/11, the tsunami in Indonesia, Hurricane Katrina and New

Orleans, AIDS and starvation in Africa, the Avian flu virus—these each raise the question, "What is needed to secure and provide for daily life?" The role of the state is to provide what individuals cannot do for themselves. Ancient Israel confronted such questions as they settled the land of Canaan. Absolute hospitality—a restoration of all people to full participation in society—was impossible without bringing the economy to a halt, causing suffering to all, and making worse the situation of those in need. Instead, the codes of Israel recall the Jubilee year and seek ways to realize the broader claim to care for those in need. This included, for example, a law for property owners to give sufficient material provisions for indentured servants at the time of their release so that they would not fall back into slavery (Deut 15:13–14). It also included a law that in harvesting owners were to leave a tithe, a tenth, so that a final harvesting could be done by the poor, by those without property—not only widows and orphans but also resident aliens (Lev 19:9). In such ways Israel sought to combine the nomadic ethic of hospitality with responsibility to create and sustain an economic order.

Similarly, Roman Catholic social thought expresses the purpose of the state as a matter of basic justice: to provide the basic or minimum conditions necessary for participation in the life of the community for all persons. Such justice is a matter of God's order, God's justice. As the prophets spoke, the measure of basic justice is the state of the poor and all in need. They cannot be sacrificed for the benefit of others. But having identified the end result, basic justice does not in itself answer what trade-offs we should make and so what policies we should pursue.[4]

For example, in terms of goals, universal health care is a matter of meeting basic human needs. In the case of catastrophic illness and injury, universal health care ensures meeting those needs that individuals cannot provide for themselves. However, the goal does not determine how this may best be done. This involves assessments about what will actually work best to create supply and meet demand, whether through a national health care system or through a free market system of health-care delivery with government incentives or subsidies so that all will be covered (if not immediately, then as soon as possible).[5]

Likewise, trade-offs are inevitable on matters of economic policies: for example, how high should interest rates be raised in order to guard against inflation and protect persons on fixed incomes when those rates come at the cost of higher unemployment and increased poverty for some? So also, international policies depend on reading of situations and a weighing of possible consequences. Contributions to debt relief for heavily indebted poor countries (HIPC) would relieve governments of debt payments that may constitute more than half of the income they collect each year. Money saved could be used for basic human services and to build essential infrastructure for the society. However, the forgiveness of debt will help the majority of people who are poor only if corruption is curbed and some basics of good government are in place.

The most difficult of choices for the citizens of a nation, though, is when—and when not—to go to war. While individuals may witness to God's kingdom by altogether renouncing the use of lethal force, states cannot do so. The state is constituted to protect its people from attack. As just war principles have put it, the use of force is just when it is to protect innocent people from harm. But here again, how do you measure and weigh the immediate consequences of death against at best probable future consequences? The war against Germany in World War II is one thing; whether to use the atomic bomb against Japan or else send hundreds of thousands of troops into hand-to-hand combat on Japanese-controlled islands is another matter. And what of Somalia, the Congo, Liberia, Sudan, Kosovo, Haiti, Afghanistan, Iraq, Iran, or Syria? As possibilities increase from nomadic encounters to modern warfare and terrorism, there is no end to weighing consequences in terms of justice.[6] Reasonable persons will disagree, but a state has to act, and citizens have to decide what citizenship requires them to do.

The conflicts of citizenship are not in opposition to hospitality; rather, hospitality is the counterpoint to citizenship. Hospitality as the care and the embrace of the stranger and those in need is the end and purpose of life in Christ, but that end is played out only in the continuum of citizenship. Christians since Augustine have stated the moral dilemma in such a life in terms of the analogy of living in two cities, the human city and the city of God. Augustine begins *The City of God* with the image of the glorious City of God. This is the city of hospitality where we are meant to live in love and peace in the light of God. We, however, also live in the human city that is moved not by hospitality and love but by power and interest. The human city is, therefore, at war within itself.

Reinhold Niebuhr phrased these two sides of life as matters of moral "man" and immoral society, of the children of light and the children of darkness.[7] But, of course, these two cities are not separate realms, one in the heavens and the other on earth, one an ideal and the other the real. Human choices are not choices between idealism and realism, between love and justice. There can be no single, simple answer to the question of how we should live faithfully as citizens. Moral discernment is rather a matter of how to live faithfully according to our ideals even while we perceive that we can act effectively only in assessing interests, possibilities, and consequences.[8]

Scripture often poses quandaries we confront and forces us into the process of moral discernment. As Kim Beckmann explored in her sermon on the question of gambling, in terms of citizenship Jesus responds to his inquisitors about whether or not to pay taxes to Caesar, saying, "Give to the emperor the things that are the emperor's, and to God the things that are God's" (Mark 12:17; also Matt 22:21; Luke 20:25). The response leaves his inquisitors amazed, confused. They do not know how to respond because they know the truth: the kingdom of God and the human city are not to be identified and yet are not two realms.

More broadly, questions of citizenship are posed whenever Scripture proclaims the kingdom of God. For example, each year the Advent lessons move from the call to repentance on the first Sunday of Advent to the announcement that the kingdom of God is given in Jesus. In each year of the lectionary, the Epistles, in turn, focus on the attitudes and intentions of Christians as they stand in the presence of God's kingdom. As these lessons variously commend a stance toward the world, they open questions of citizenship and Christian responsibility in particular. The questions of citizenship are broad and diverse. What are the responsibilities of citizenship, of not only paying taxes but keeping informed, voting, speaking up, and making political contributions? What then of specific issues: questions of rights (from free speech to the right to bear arms), the separation of church and state (including the question of teaching theories of intelligent design alongside evolution in science curriculum), freedom of choice (as in matters deeply informed by conscience such as abortion or same-sex marriage)? And when is the state so fallen and corrupted that Christians are called to prophetic witness and living as a faithful counter-society, even to the point of martyrdom?[9]

Citizenship, it may be said, is the continuum on which the notes of hospitality are played. In turn, prayer and worship inform and shape our response as citizens; they are central practices of Christian citizenship. So, too, forgiveness and reconciliation are practices essential to forming a city, as are the way we form our particular households. As our account of practices suggests, practices of faith together serve to orchestrate the play of the different parts of our life that they may be concordant, whole rather than fragmented parts. But like a song, practices are not some thematic generalization but are given in the play. They are not a program for preaching but a means of focusing in order to explore and discern the word of God for our life in light of Scripture.

REVERENCE FOR CREATION

In the reach of hospitality, if citizenship is the horizon of our actions toward other persons, reverence for creation is the response beyond ourselves to the natural world.[10] As a practice, reverence for creation has been especially expressed in hymnody, in songs of praise. For example, the *Benedicite* (*A Song of Creation* from the Apocrypha *Song of the Three Young Men* 33–55) was sung in the Church of England at Morning Prayer, beginning with the 1549 Prayer Book. A similar sense of reverence toward nature is expressed by Francis of Assisi and his hymn calling for brother sun and sister moon to praise the Lord.[11] Christians revere nature as a creation that is cause for awe, given its power and magnificence, that, in turn, fosters a sense of human limit and frailty. As God is the creator, the creation glorifies God; it witnesses to God's glory, majesty, power, and goodness.

Like the stranger, nature calls us beyond ourselves. Reverence for creation, as with hospitality, begins with recognition and acknowledgment. Human life stands as part of creation, dependent on the created order whose purpose is beyond human understanding. Nature provides the very conditions that make possible human life. But it should never be understood as created for the sake of humanity, as if humans were at the center of the world and as if all of creation were for our enjoyment and satisfaction. Creation has its own beauty and goodness that demands recognition. In such acknowledgment humans are "decentered."[12] They can no longer assume that they are at the center of the world. Rather, they are turned outward in thanks and praise and in love and care.

This move from reverence to care is reflected in the first creation account in Genesis that begins Scripture and is itself something of a hymn to creation. God creates light from darkness and the heavens above the seas, separates land from water, and fills the earth with plants, fish, and animals of every kind. And God declares that it is good, indeed very good. Humans are then created as part of creation. What is distinctive about humans is that they are created in the image of God. Like God they are to love and care for creation. In this sense they are God's representatives with the power to rule over the world, to be stewards, in order that God's will may be done.[13]

Before the twentieth century, reverence and care for nature were highly circumscribed. Human life seemed fragile in the face of nature. Famine, plague, and natural disasters threatened human existence. Practices of worship expressed the sense of awe and of our dependence. Care for creation was narrowly circumscribed to such matters as treating animals well and not beating beasts of burden. It was impossible to imagine that humans could affect the course of nature, much less manage nature as one's own in order to increase productivity and maximize benefits for human consumption. That changed with the scientific discoveries and technological advances in the nineteenth and twentieth centuries.

In the nineteenth century the discovery of the relationship between disease and sanitation was the most significant factor in stabilizing and raising the levels of human population on the earth. In the twentieth century the possibility of controlling nature followed such advances as the understanding of disease, the development of vaccines and antibiotics, the understanding of genetics, and the development of genetically selected or modified seeds that resulted in the Green Revolution.

Technological advances also meant that nature could be exploited for profit, from beaver belts to the harvesting of aboriginal forests, from fossil fuels to precious metals. Waters could be dammed so that land could be settled and energy produced. Wetlands and floodplains could be drained and sold for farming or for building new towns and cities. What had appeared to be limitless suddenly became threatened. Humans were able to destroy ecological environments, terminate animal species, deplete natural resources, and in the process change the environment as a whole. Global warming is only the most recent sign of such power. Human beings have the power to destroy creation itself, at least as we know it.[14] Stewardship could no longer be viewed as husbandry but could only mean the care of creation itself.

The practice of reverence for creation raises moral questions not unlike those of citizenship. What are the tradeoffs between the care of nature and human well-being? How do you choose between jobs in mining or lumbering and preserving nature, between oil exploration and production and the possible destruction of the environment? Who is to bear the burden of environmentalism—developed countries or undeveloped countries, workers or investors, the rich or the poor? And what is politically possible, enforceable, especially when the environment requires action among the nations of the world?

Like the practice of citizenship, the practice of reverence for creation moves between individual disciplines and corporate politics. Our practice of reverence shapes our relationship to nature, bears witness to the larger society, and effects change. Individual choices regarding consumption, recycling, where we live and how we travel, size of homes and forms of recreation make a difference. At the same time—as a matter of citizenship—care of creation requires corporate action. Unless provisions are made, the poor can't afford to make decisions and purchases based on the good of the environment and too many others simply won't change voluntarily.

Altogether the practices of Christian faith form a vision of the Christian life. Again, like a set of lenses, practices focus attention on the specific actions and the fundamental attitudes, dispositions, and intentions that constitute Christian faith and life. Such an account of the practices of Christian faith is needed if preaching isn't to become captive to particular traditions of preaching, the specific interests of the preacher, or narrow concerns of distinct biblical texts. Other accounts or variations of this account of Christian practices may also serve in providing a larger vision of the Christian life; however, the account must be both concrete and not too broad. Too many lenses fragment light and vision.

Finally, as we have tried to emphasis, practices shouldn't be confused with what should be preached. Preaching as proclaiming the word of God in a particular time and place means that preaching must arise concretely in engagement of Scripture and the immediate life of the gathered community. What then does preaching for moral discernment through the lenses of these practices look like? Here is an example drawn from a different tradition (Episcopal rather than Lutheran) and offered in a different context (a seminary chapel in a suburb of Washington DC, rather than a rural parish in Northern Michigan).

The intent of both preachers is not to avoid the responsibility of the pulpit simply by tossing the quandary back in the lap of listeners. Instead, both preachers seek to enable a fresh hearing of a familiar biblical text in order to further moral discernment in the community. Again, homiletical analysis will be deferred until that topic is addressed (in the next two chapters). As with the sermon

"Is It Lawful for Christians to Gamble," note how moral discernment is evoked through the play between the open-endedness of the narrative of Scripture and the open-endedness of our lives. More behind the scenes, framing and forming the sermon, are understandings of the practices of the Christian life.

Most explicitly, this sermon explores what is meant and required by hospitality in order to form the household of God. Observe as well how the practices of "prayer and worship" and (less overtly, but nonetheless clearly) "forgiveness and reconciliation" form essential background for the shift of gestalt that the preacher seeks to engender. While "reverence for creation" does not figure as a lens here, there are certainly echoes and implications of questions concerning "citizenship."

—◯—

SHOCK THERAPY[15]

Text: "Listen to me, all of you, and understand: there is nothing outside a person that by going in can defile, but the things that come out are what defile" (Mark 7:14–23).

Jesus deals in shock therapy. He has a way of throwing high explosives into a conversation: a parable of a prodigal son, a Good Samaritan, an unjust steward. Or he just plain says it: "Do not worry about your life...consider the lilies of the field" (Matt 6:25, 28); "Let the dead bury their own dead" (Matt 8:22; Luke 9:60); "The sabbath was made for humankind, and not humankind for the sabbath" (Mark 2:27). Or today: "There is nothing outside a person that by going in can defile, but the things that come out are what defile" (Mark 7:15).

Here is a verbal bomb that we are invited to catch, the word of God, cast across cultural divides. Jesus has this way of revealing the rules of our game and the high stakes that we may forfeit. Perhaps that is why his verbal explosions are so revealing. They make us rethink everything.

We are celebrating here in this community, in this chapel, the beginning of the second week of Black History Month, really begun last Friday evening with two hours of African drumming, thurible incensing, black preaching, gospel singing, every voice lifting, Eucharist making.

- Why, we might ask, why was this an exceptional service?
- Why, we might ask, do we have Black History Month in the first place? Why are these differences in worship important?
- In demanding change or in resisting change, are we not holding on to externals?
- Are not our attachments and commitments like the Pharisees in their clinging to dietary laws?
- Are we dividing the world between clean and unclean, pure and impure?

But this is all too broad and abstract. What does our Scripture for today say about race, worship, about a gospel that is multi-ethnic and multi-cultural?

I am drawn back to my own past. In worship and friendships, through child-raising, as member and warden and teacher and occasional preacher, one of my greatest joys was sharing in the life of a parish for some eighteen years while I taught at Seabury-Western Theological Seminary. I recall our relationship with the one Caribbean–African-American Episcopal congregation.

We had studied the history of the four Episcopal congregations in the city and how they reflected the history of racial division. The Anglicans from the Islands had formed a congregation on their own side of town that expressed their traditions. The church was a center of the community. It was theirs. It was where they were accepted and responsible and in charge of their lives. They welcomed the African-Americans into the parish but a bit on their own terms.

On the other side of town near the lake was our parish. In the 1930s it had been the pro-cathedral for the diocese. There were a few African-Americans; most had come into the community as students or as young professionals and were not part of the significant Caribbean or African-American community in the city.

We and the other two Anglo parishes wanted to work more closely together with the Caribbean–African-American parish in order to support one another while respecting our history and needs. We wanted to be more one body in Christ. Together the four parishes did a joint vestry retreat with then bishop of Chicago, Frank Griswold. We celebrated together Epiphany as a non-Sunday major feast. We had celebrated confirmations together. Some personal relationships developed. The four rectors became more significantly connected. But our peoples and parishes remained worlds apart. It was difficult to sustain initiatives, especially when each parish had its own significant challenges.

To paraphrase the highly priestly prayer from the Gospel of John (John 17:11, 21), why, I've asked, could we not be One so that the world might know that God has sent Christ that we all might be One as the Father and the Son are One?

I hear Jesus' shock therapy: there is nothing that can defile. Don't let history and ritual separate you. But then I think what it is that defiles and whether the outer and inner can be so neatly separated.

The Caribbean blacks and the African-American blacks who came to our Anglo parish for worship would join us in the shadow of Gothic columns, hear the Skinner organ and feel its reverberations silence everything else until the boys or girls choir sounded a high English voice as they led the parade through the congregation to the choir stalls and the high altar. Everything pressed against our guests saying, "You're out of place. This is not your place."

In their generosity our Caribbean and African-American guests would graciously accept our welcome, just as we appreciated their warmth when we joined them for worship. But they had no desire to form a single worshipping community any more than we did. Visiting was one thing, but forming a common worship community was something else.

Our styles of worship—and more importantly our power to make decisions about the shape of our liturgy—was part of the larger power of shaping our mission and ministry: opportunities for our children, forms of education, strategies for renewal and evangelism for ourselves and for our surrounding communities.

Neither of us could let go of our particular community with its culturally specific forms of worship, programs, and priorities. In fact, to do so would stain—defile—our commitments and identity. But Jesus' words come back again: "There is nothing outside a person that by going in can defile, but the things that come out are what defile" (Mark 7:15). The power of this declaration is its eschatological character. In God's kingdom nothing outside persons can defile, stain, constrict, or deny the faith that is in them. All that divides us will fall away, and we will be One as the Father and the Son are One. But forming a community of faith this side of the kingdom is of another order. For those growing in faith and, more significantly, for sharing faith with others, the external, what is outside, the culturally specific, makes all the difference.

Now we are in Paul's realm (which we are now reading in our Sunday lectionary) as he seeks to offer guidance to the Corinthians. Some lines can be clearly drawn, as when our worship has turned from Christ to our particular community with our own particular leader—evangelical, liberal, black church or white church. We belong to Christ and therefore we belong to each other, to bear each other's burdens, to respect and support each other in our common mission and ministry. But at other points we can't simply draw neat lines. We seek to discern and balance different needs for the sake of each person and community that they might grow in faith this side of the kingdom.

What makes the call for a multi-ethnic and multi-racial community so difficult is that we tend to think in terms of a grand idea, an eschatological image, that we will be one beyond our particularity. But as we believe in the incarnation and the resurrection of the dead, we don't exist apart from our particular cultures and traditions. A multi-ethnic and multi-racial community might rather mean a community of diverse worship: not an amalgam of bits and pieces but worship that is truly different where all are at times hosts and at times guests. This too is appealing, but we don't often look at what such a community requires.

What is dominant at our seminary is a style we might call Anglican worship, Book of Common Prayer worship, or the English tradition. The style is given in the Benedictine shape of the Book of Common Prayer and in its language, which we inherit from Thomas Cranmer and the Elizabethan settlement. In this community we often then have show and tell: we show our difference by offering music and worship that reflects our own homes and traditions—Evangelical East Africans, Anglo-Catholic East Africans, African-Americans, Native Americans, Hispanic, Presbyterian, Lutheran, all with greater particularity than these labels suggest.

But we can't have truly a multi-ethnic and multi-racial community of worship unless we have here particular communities who are not guests. This can't happen where only one or two are gathered together. It requires a sufficient mass of like-minded people or, better, a critical mass of a particular traditioned people with power to enact and celebrate their lives. This need to have a critical mass with power to enact and celebrate their life is why African-Americans turned to black power and sought to develop strong and healthy black institutions.

Such a multi-ethnic, multi-racial seminary community would not assume any single unity or understanding any more than we have a common identity and understanding between different generations of students or between men and women. Rather, the unity we are called to in Christ is more respect of difference and acknowledgment of lack of understanding. In this way we can begin to support each other in our differences and separateness while also joining together where there is need and common mission and ministry.

What this requires is not clear:

- What is a critical mass of African-American students and faculty and administrators?
- Should students be integrated in advising or should there be a single advising group of African-American students?
- Or should the burden of association rest upon African-American students beyond and in addition to the regular round of activities and demands?
- Should there be regular services that are African-American in style?

- But then whose style? Which style?
- Should we have an all African-American worship team?
- Does the curriculum—the order of courses we take—create or assume a dominant Anglo reality by not addressing the different contexts of mission and ministry?
- What about closer relationships with Howard Divinity School?
- Should African-American students take courses there as a necessary part of their curriculum? Should there be some joint program?

In the midst of such questions is the question of power. There can be no multi-ethnic and multi-racial community without the full integrity of each community, and that means critical mass with power to enact and to celebrate their life. This requires in the community as a whole respect for difference, toleration for ambiguity, and the danger of separation. But any other basis for community is accommodation and subtle forms of assimilation.

Jesus' shock therapy startles us awake. "There is nothing outside a person that by going in can defile, but the things that come out are what defile" (Mark 7:15). "All these evil things come from within, and they defile a person" (Mark 7:23).

This judgment calls us to conversion, to wake up, and to love beyond ourselves. Whether fear or comfort or simply over-identification with what we know as good, hanging on uncritically to our own forms of worship or hanging on to the ways things are apart from the needs of others is idolatrous. But the judgment against purity laws and all forms of idolatry does not tell us what to do.

Our loves and hopes, fear and trust are shaped by our deep participation in particular communities. God comes not simply in breaking boundaries and welcoming the other as guest. To receive God in the other requires giving space and power to communities beyond our own. Only then may we hear each other's needs and see what God is calling us to do together.

—⌒—

The challenge of preaching comes from the fact that bearing the Gospel in word is an art rather than a science. The art of preaching for moral discernment is a learned rhetorical skill that begins with reading text and context through the lenses of the practices of faith. And so we need to attend to the rhetorical strategies so that the preacher can engage those who would hear.

To think about what needs to come together in any preaching—and here specifically in preaching moral discernment—can be overwhelming if not paralyzing. For the experienced preacher, like any artist, the elements that inform a sermon come together naturally and often intuitively. Attention, though, to the parts can aid the experienced preacher; for the new preacher it is critical. To complete our rendering of what is required to engage the crises and quandaries before us and to form our lives in faith, we turn now to address the question, "How will it preach?"

Notes

1. For a historical-critical account of Jubilee in Scripture and a review of literature, see Sharon H. Ringe, *Jesus, Liberation, and the Biblical Jubilee* (Philadelphia: Fortress, 1985).

2. Emmanuel Levinas, *Totality and Infinity: An Essay on Exteriority*, trans. Alphonso Lingis (Pittsburgh, PA: Duquesne University Press, 1969), esp. 187–247. See also Thomas W. Ogletree, *Hospitality to the Stranger* (Philadelphia: Fortress, 1985), 35–63; Edward Farley, *Good and Evil*, 31–46; Timothy F. Sedgwick, *The Christian Moral Life* (Grand Rapids, MI: Eerdmans, 1999), 53–101; Christine D. Pohl, *Making Room: Recovering Hospitality as a Christian Tradition* (Grand Rapids, MI: Eerdmans, 1999).

3. Sedgwick, *The Christian Moral Life*, 77–94.

4. See the National Conference of Catholic Bishops, *Economic Justice for All* (Washington, DC: NCCB, 1986), esp. paras. 61–95.

5. See *On Moral Medicine*, 947–973; also see Cynthia B. Cohen, et al., *Faithful Living Faithful Dying* (Harrisburg, PA: Morehouse, 2000), 99–111; Lisa Sowle Cahill, "National and International Health Access Reform," in *Theological Bioethics* (Washington, DC: Georgetown University Press, 2005), 131–68.

6. See, for example, the National Council of Catholic Bishops, *The Challenge of Peace* (Washington, DC: NCCB, 1983), paras. 70–110; James Turner Johnson, *Just War Tradition and the Restraint of War* (Princeton, NJ: Princeton University Press, 1981); Michael Walzer, *Just and*

Unjust Wars (New York: Basic Books, 1992); Michael Ignatieff, *The Lesser Evil: Political Ethics in an Age of Terror* (Princeton, NJ: Princeton University Press, 2004); Martin L. Cook, *The Moral Warrior: Ethics and Service in the U.S. Military* (Albany, NY: SUNY, 2004); Edward LeRoy Long, Jr., *Facing Terrorism: Responding as Christians* (Louisville, KY: Westminster John Knox, 2004).

7. Reinhold Niebuhr, *Moral Man and Immoral Society* (New York: Charles Scribner's Sons, 1932) and *The Children of Light and the Children of Darkness* (New York: Charles Scribner's Sons, 1944).

8. See Max Weber's classic essay, "Politics as Vocation," in *From Max Weber: Essays in Sociology*, ed. H. H. Gerth and C. Wright Mills (New York: Oxford, 1946), 77–128.

9. The most powerful contemporary voice claiming Christians are to form an alternative society is Stanley Hauerwas. See Hauerwas and William H. Willimon, *Resident Aliens* (Nashville, TN: Abingdon, 1989) and Hauerwas, *After Christendom?* (Nasvhille, TN: Abingdon, 1991).

10. For a history of the development of environmental ethics, see Roderick Frazier Nash, *The Rights of Nature: A History of Environmental Ethics* (Madison, WI: University of Wisconsin Press, 1989).

11. On the *Benedicite*, see Marion J. Hatchett, *Commentary on the American Prayer Book* (Minneapolis: Seabury Press, 1980), 113. For Francis of Assisi's hymn see *The Hymnal 1982* (New York: Church Publishing, 1982), 406, 407.

12. On nature and the decentering of the self, see James M. Gustafson, *A Sense of the Divine: The Natural Environment from a Theological Perspective* (Cleveland, OH: Pilgrim, 1994).

13. Image (*tselm*) and likeness (*demut*) are nearly synonymous. In Hebrew they convey representation: humankind is a "representation of God who is like God in certain respects." The author of this passage from Genesis repeats this idea, first in summary form (Gen 5:1–3) and then as the reason for respect of all human life (Gen 9:6). See Anthony A. Hoekama, *Created in God's Image* (Grand Rapids, MI: Eerdmans, 1986), 13. As Albert Gelin says, "derived from the theme of the image [of God]" we are to "imitate God in his battle against evil, in his labor, and by the humble reproduction of God's activity." Albert Gelin, *The Concept of Man in the Bible*, trans. D. M. Murphy (London: G. Chapman, 1968), 34, 35.

14. See James Gustave Speth, *Red Sky at Morning: America and the Crisis of the Global Environment* (New Haven, CT: Yale University Press, 2004); Al Gore, *An Inconvenient Truth* (Emmaus, PA: Rodale, 2006).

15. This sermon was preached at Virginia Theological Seminary in Alexandria, Virginia, on February 8, 2006, by Timothy Sedgwick.

CHAPTER 5

Tension and *Telos*

A CONTINUING CONVERSATION between the open-ended narratives of Scripture and experience, focused through the interpretive lenses of Christian moral practices—all this is essential in preaching that fosters moral discernment. But it is not enough. A conversation that leads toward discernment must be kindled in the community. Preaching moral discernment cannot be a matter of conclusions reached in the preacher's study.

Thesis 5: Preaching for moral discernment needs to directly undertake the adventure it seeks to articulate.

The philosopher Ludwig Wittgenstein once described language as "a toolbox."[1] By this he meant that language patterns well-suited for some purposes are inept for others. (Hammers are ideal for joining boards with nails, but useless for cutting boards apart. Emotionally neutral language is effective for dispensing information, but inadequate for expressing affection.) Wittgenstein's observation has relevance for preachers. Yes, preaching the Gospel always entails announcing the good news of God's love to a world that needs, misunderstands, resists, and suffers for want of it. Yet this universal word is never generic: it addresses hearers in particular circumstances that vary vastly.

Preachers (including those whom we come upon in Scripture) undertake a wide range of purposes. They proclaim and celebrate, inform and educate, console and reassure, confront and challenge, inspire and enlist, stir imagination and invite reflection, rebuke and remonstrate, absolve and urge amendment of life, evoke consensus and articulate resolve, form character and foster discernment. Clearly, the requirements for effective preaching in one context do not transpose directly into another. In terms of preaching strategy, then, what do all such sermons have in common? And how does preaching toward moral discernment find its distinctive place in relation to the strategies it shares with other modes of preaching?

LISTENING AND SPEAKING

Regardless of focus and intent, all Gospel preaching must be informed by both hermeneutical listening and homiletical listening.

* By hermeneutical listening we mean the listening necessary for hearing the Word that needs to be preached. Hermeneutical listening requires disciplined exegesis informed by continuing conversations among voices in Scripture, tradition, current culture, and one's own experience. Hermeneutical listening enters deeply into a "spirited" conversation through which God's leading is revealed in process, not simply received as pronouncement.

* By homiletical listening we mean listening for words that will most effectively engage those before whom God's Word will be proclaimed.

As they prepare sermons, preachers are listening, both hermeneutically and homiletically, for an interplay between what may be understood as the *tension* and *telos* that are present in Scripture and in our lives.[2] By depicting and conveying tension, effective Gospel sermons lead listeners into a *telos*, a purpose that is "larger than life" as currently envisioned and experienced. A faithful re-presenting of God's redemptive grace has the feel of a journey through the wilderness, from bondage toward freedom, from darkness into light.

"Tension" in preaching honors the fact that life is never an easy, seamless move from "once upon a time" to "happily ever after." Conflict and complexity, change and challenge are endemic to life. Any preaching not deeply in touch with showering sparks of tension will not touch lives, hearts, and situations with the Gospel.

Tension, however, only has meaning as it is related to a *telos*. Meaning-laden living is always going somewhere: headed in a direction (the "holy calling" of God in Christ, [2 Tim 1:9]), intent upon achieving a significant purpose ("Your kingdom come" (Matt 6:10]). Achievements, failures, detours and delays, plans and ideals, reality checks and readjustments: the goal-intending, trajectory-plotting quality of Gospel preaching is not the antithesis of tension but its complement.

Think about sermons you have heard (or preached) that you regard as "good" or "bad." Regardless of specific purpose, sermons you deem "successful," we wager, are ones that have embodied an interplay of *tension* and *telos* in a manner appropriate to the particular occasion. Sermons you judge "unsuccessful," we have a hunch are ones that have lacked such interplay.

The "tension and *telos*" character of preaching is essential, whether the preacher is seeking to inspire and enlist, to comfort and assure, or to challenge and confront. All preaching intends to move listeners along: to leave them off at a different place than wherever they were when they came aboard the sermon process. A sermon uttered in the darkness of despair needs to light a torch of hope on the far horizon. A sermon set forth in the midst of complacency needs to sound a trumpet. A sermon proclaimed in the midst of intellectual confusion needs to plant signs along a twisted path.

This "tensive/telic" character of good preaching suggests several practical corollaries:

- Preaching is an oral/aural art form. Insight and understanding cannot be revealed "all at once" (as in a painting or sculpture) but only in an unfolding sequence.[3]

- Good preaching issues invitations; it does not impose edicts. The Gospel gives its listeners space to weigh and consider, resist or embrace the implications of life made new in Jesus Christ.

- Preaching exemplifies the dynamics of a journey in faith shared by community and preacher alike—an ever-deepening discovery—rather than an achievement fixed and finished.

- Preaching has an eschatological character: it celebrates expansively the trajectory of God's creating-redeeming acts. The Gospel depicts not a straightforward incarnational rescue, but a mysterious process of cosmic transformation, at once already accomplished yet still yearned for because imperfectly realized.

PREACHING MORAL DISCERNMENT

How can these principles be further specified to foster moral discernment from the pulpit? There are, we believe, six features that characterize such preaching:

1. A nonpartisan and non-polarizing delineation of the presenting quandary/crisis and its moral dimensions.

2. A theological exploration of how God is present in a quandary/crisis and what God is calling us to do in the midst of moral conflict.

3. A listening to Scripture and the moral discernment it depicts by means of value pictures, behavior patterns, and reasoning processes.

4. An interpretation of the quandary/crisis we presently face in light of relevant Christian practices.

5. An emphasis on corporate accountability and response.

6. An integrated unfolding of these explorations (by means of metaphor, narrative, and argument) through a "tension/*telos*" trajectory that is deliberative, dialogical, and mimetic.

It is unrealistic to accomplish all of these goals in every sermon, but all will be incorporated into a preaching rhythm, deployed over weeks and months through the liturgical year. As indicated earlier, what we are primarily concerned about in moral discernment preaching is more akin to fitness training than to the kind of "desperate measures" necessary in an emergency room.[4] Let's consider each of these distinctive foci in turn.

Discernment preaching delineates the moral dimensions of the quandary and crisis

"You can't have your cake and eat it too." The familiar adage names a fact of life we acknowledge in the abstract. All value choices involve selection and rejection. Every gain is attended by loss. Yet who of us has not tried (perhaps half-consciously) to get it all for nothing? Hence the long shelf life of the lowly proverb!

Moral conflict stands at the heart of the decisions that form our lives. Should I move from my present location in order to follow greater opportunities for work or to provide for better education of my children, or should I remain within the web of geographical and social relationships that have sustained my life in order to care for my aging parents? Should I undergo chemotherapy to prolong my life or should I refuse treatment so that I can live most fully the days that are given to me? At the risk of losing privacy and civil rights, should we, for the sake of security, support the Patriot Act? Goods are often in conflict: hard choices must be made. We cannot have our cake and eat it too.

Of course we hope that if we marshal the evidence, weigh the factors, reflect on our principles, and pray for God's will, moral ambiguity will be, at last, resolved. In the midst of real quandaries, however, faithful persons may agree on what stands "beyond the pale" but still will disagree about what exactly should be done.

The first task of the preacher, therefore, may be to help a community come to realize that moral discernment involves recognizing and exploring moral quandaries more than removing or resolving them. Moral weighing and wrestling are not necessarily manifestations of moral weakness. In fact, moral and spiritual certitude is often counterproductive to respect for others, and to the disciplined work of discernment that people of faith are continually called to undertake.

Moral discernment preaching explores the question of what God is calling us to do in the midst of moral quandaries/crises

When confronted with moral quandaries, conflicting descriptions, and moral claims, it is not enough to ask simply, "What would Jesus do?", or as abbreviated on bracelets, "WWJD?"[5]

The implicit assumption in "WWJD?" is that Christians have access to "insider information" (derived from biblical texts, church pronouncements, or special revelation) that renders rigorous moral wrestling moot. It should hardly be surprising that the "answers" often received from such "spiritual discernment" are the very answers to which the seeker was predisposed. Bumper sticker theology may catch the eye and ear, and infuse an instant "buzz," but it provides little guidance for hands and feet, and energy insufficient for patient, painstaking labor over the long haul. Much of the "moral insight" derived from "seeking God's will" gives little more in the way of dependable direction.

But one of us saw a bumper sticker recently that calls into question the summary dismissal of the last paragraph. It went like this: "Who would Jesus bomb?" A shrill sound bite from a frustrated pacifist, perhaps; nonetheless it posed succinctly the sort of discerning question that is involved in framing the issue theologically. In a phrase, the bumper sticker crystallized the claim that for Christian communities more is required in the moral assessment of national defense policy than calculating the relative costs and benefits of terrorist deterrence and collateral damage. The bumper sticker challenges the assumption that the right or duty of self-defense is self-evident or at least unexceptionable. God may have something else in mind for us. The way of the cross might in some circumstances have serious, even literal implications.

The rule of God, announced by Jesus as "at hand," signals the end of moral discernment as narrowly a matter of individual and collective interests—whether the issue is war and peace, private ownership and social responsibility, or the right to life and the right to choice. Exploring moral quandaries theologically asks questions about God's purposes and about holiness of life. Preaching for moral discernment must do the same.

Moral discernment preaching listens to Scripture and the discernment it offers through value pictures, behavior patterns, and reasoning processes

Scripture is not a moral maxim manual. Instead, Scripture witnesses to life lived in relationship to God. It is as inconceivable for Christians "to do justice, and to love kindness, and to walk humbly with your God"(Mic 6:8) apart from appropriating the full scope of biblical witness as it is for physicists or flautists to develop their professional skills by apprenticing themselves to a single mentor.

There are many moral issues that the Scriptures do not directly or definitively address. Even when a clear majority of voices in Scripture and tradition speak in striking unity (as they do, for instance, regarding communal responsibility for the economically disadvantaged), there is still hard work to be done in moving from purposes or principles to particular policies or practices. What the Scriptures do for moral decision-making is to offer pictures of the moral life, patterns of moral behavior, and processes of moral reasoning.[6]

Pictures of the moral life: examples, metaphors, visions of life lived in relationship to God that are both positive and negative

"A picture is worth a thousand words," the old adage says, and it is seldom more applicable than in the area of moral discernment, since the process of discernment is as much about evoking the imagination of what life can and should be as it is about gathering information, determining possibilities, assessing obligations, and weighing consequences. Take, for example, the Garden of Eden where Adam and Eve live for each other, naked and not ashamed (Gen 2:25). Consider love's delight in The Song of Songs. Or look at the vision of Jubilee where all are forgiven their debts so that all can participate fully as members of society (Lev 25:1–2a, 8–10); Ezekiel's discovery that dry bones can live (chapter 37); Isaiah's promise of "new heavens and a new earth" where Jerusalem will be restored as a city in which there will be no more weeping but only the sound of joy (Isa 65); and Jesus' proclamation that the poor are blessed and those who weep now will laugh (Luke 6:21).

Such visions are often developed in critique. Think of Matthew's contrasting pictures (in chapter 14) of the palace banquet that Herod puts on for his cronies that leads, through levels of lust, physical and political, to the procuring of the head of John the Baptist on a platter. Hard upon this grisly scene follows the simple feast of bread and fish that Jesus and his disciples provide in the wilderness for thousands of ordinary folks. Or think of Nathan's deft characterization of David's preemptory exercise of political power (in taking Bathsheba and murdering Uriah) as that of a rich man with abundant herds stealing and slaughtering a lamb that was the beloved pet of a poor family (2 Sam 12). Consider Amos's plumb line (Amos 7:7–9), Jesus' parable of the rich fool (Luke 12:13–21), or the use of armor put on for conflict or weights set aside for running a race in Ephesians (6:10–17).

Such pictures in Scripture do more than inspire feelings and prompt action. They serve as centering interpretive signs, often in the midst of situations where factors are complex and conflicted and the impulse to resort to self-interest is palpable. Moral discernment preaching will draw heavily for inspiration on the visions of life in God as imaged in the Scriptures.

Patterns of moral behavior: commandments and counsels, entreaties and injunctions

Often, in an attempt to put forth a Christian moral vision as "objective"—fixed for all persons, times, and places—patterns of behavior are put forth as "rules and regulations." It is said rhetorically, for example: "At Sinai, God did not promulgate Ten Suggestions, but Ten Commandments—eternal laws admitting no exceptions." Without entering deeply into a debate over what is involved in moral objectivity, we want to propose that "patterns" is a more fruitful way of describing what is advanced by biblical authors as morally normative, rather than behaviorally definitive checklists of "Do's and Don't's."

The Ten Commandments, in fact, are a set of absolute demands to act with consistency of intent. These describe the covenant relationship between human persons and God. What that requires in specific situations where these demands conflict is, however, not always clear—hence the conversation in Scripture and in tradition.[7] Similarly, the Beatitudes and much of Matthew's Sermon on the Mount (Matt 5–7) and Luke's Sermon on the Plain (Luke 6:17–46), Paul's depiction of the gifts of the Holy Spirit (Gal 5:22–23), or the practical manifestations of love that "never ends" (1 Cor 13:8) depict a pattern of purposes, attitudes, and dispositions. Less imaginative than pictures, these patterns depict what is entailed as an essential orientation for Christians undertaking moral discernment.

Like the biblical pictures described previously, the Ten Commandments and other commandments, counsels, entreaties, and injunctions focus the work of discernment but by no means do they render it unnecessary. Life should be valued and never murdered, but when is the taking of a life "murder"? Love "bears all things, believes all things, hopes all things, endures all things" (1 Cor 13:7), but how that applies for those who are subjected to domestic abuse is another question altogether. Preachers need to draw upon such patterns and engage in analogous patterning as well as picturing, but that still is not all that they need to do.

Processes of moral reasoning—accounts of the steps in deliberation fostered in or undertaken by faith communities

Certain texts—and especially the Epistles, as the letters of the early Church seeking to live faithfully in light of Christ—offer invaluable windows into communities that are deeply engaged in the process of moral discernment. While the issues on the table in biblical texts are never "just the same" as ours (and sometimes nowhere close), these vivid vignettes of moral deliberation, if considered carefully, provide as much if not more help for preachers and congregations committed to discernment than the more immediately obvious pictures and patterns.

Examples of "processing" have the potential to deeply inform our immediate challenges to moral discernment: attending, for example, to how the Jerusalem Council (Acts 15) works through "the Gentile question"; or how Paul addresses the matter of circumcision (Gal 5–6), the practice of table fellowship, the exercise of spiritual gifts, the vexing dilemma posed in "meat offered to idols" (1 Cor 9–14), the concerns of steward-ship in the collection of resources for famine relief (Rom 15; 2 Cor 9); or how in the Letter of James the community wrestles with the seductive temptation to the power of riches.

Moral discernment preaching sees moral quandaries and crises in light of Christian practices

Broader still than pictures of value, patterns of behavior, or even processes of moral reasoning are the practices we have discussed: prayer and worship, forgiveness and reconciliation, householding, hospitality, citizenship, and reverence for creation. Together these present a unified picture of the Christian moral life that makes sense of the particular pictures, patterns, and processes in Scrip-ture. They offer something akin to a description of "Christian moral wholeness or wellness."

Healthy living habits are themselves, generally speaking, the first line of prevention and defense against bodily breakdown and crisis (in the American usage of that term). One can only imagine how many moral crises, as well, could be/have been avoided by a kind of "preventive moral maintenance." Yet moral crises (even more than medical crises) come regardless of how fit a "body" may be. Indeed, a primary fruit (and index) of moral/spiritual health in a morally wounded world (infested, as it is, by principalities and powers) may be the provoking of contin-ually more serious crises (in the earlier sense of the term, i.e. a "turning point"). All we need to do is reference the life of Jesus in this regard.

In such crises the practices we have begun to describe can function diagnostically as lenses of analysis. These are especially needed in highly charged social situations and environments where anxiety quickly turns hysterical and debate easily degener-ates into polarizing diatribe. It is not about right worship and strict observance but about how prayer and worship draw us into relation to God and more broadly about hospitality (Matt 6). It is not about our notions of family and children but about what enduring love means for households (Mark 10:6–9; 19:11–15). The preacher's task (along with employing pictures, patterns, and processes) is to bring particular quandaries and Christian practices into conversation, fostering discernment of what is involved in the quandaries and crises of our lives.

Moral discernment preaching emphasizes corporate accountability and response

"Many members, yet one body" (1 Cor 12:20): the Pauline notion carries little currency in a society where individualism is rampant. How hard it is in the faith community to uphold and sustain a way of being together so foreign to the individualism that pervades contemporary life. We do not easily check patterns of social interaction when we enter the sanctuary; nor do we easily translate the patterns of covenantal care embedded in the language of worship into these same patterns of social interactions.

Yet Christian moral discernment both presupposes and calls community members into the ever-deepening practical realization that we are fundamentally responsible for and accountable to one another in the body of Christ. Under the influence of consumer-driven cultural forces, claims on behalf of "individual conscience" can seem self-evidently appropriate. "I can't legislate for you, but I am entitled to my own opinion" is often a discussion-stifling "last word." Instead, pulpit space needs to become conversation-convening space: a space that engenders not so much tolerance for "majority rule" as a recognition of the fact that we may not even know our own minds until we listen to each other and learn to hear our deepest selves in what others say. Preaching toward moral discernment will thus call persons into community to share and test the spirits in order to discern the spirit of God (1 John 4:1). To moral discernment no less than any other activity in the body of Christ, "the eye cannot say to the hand, 'I have no need of you'" (1 Cor 12).

For effective moral discernment preaching these five features will be shaped by a palpable sense of tension and *telos*. Moral quandaries must be revealed in tension with the will of God. Value pictures, behavior patterns, and reasoning processes in Scripture must present the character of our life in God as that arises from the crises and quandaries the Scripture writers confront. Crises and quandaries stand always in a dialectical relationship with a vision of faithful Christian living described in terms of the practices of the Christian life. Finally, individual and community must be drawn together in the process of moral discernment; again, between the two are tensions in the midst of which emerges God's call and promise to us for the conversion and flourishing of our life together in God.

What still remains to be explored is how these five features of moral discernment preaching may be actually preached. To this we now turn in the next chapter.

Notes

1. Ludwig Wittgenstein, *Philosophical Investigations*, ed. G. E. M. Anscomb (New York: Prentice Hall, 1999), aphorism 11.

2. As first articulated in Aristotle's *Poetics* in terms of plot, Paul Ricoeur develops the understanding of narrative as a matter of emplotment of contrary elements so as to integrate them in terms of some kind of identity. See *Time and Narrative*, 3 vols. (Chicago: The University of Chicago Press, 1984, 1985, 1989), esp. vol. 1; and *Oneself as Another* (Chicago: The University of Chicago Press, 1992), 140–47.

3. On orality, see Walter J. Ong, *Orality and Literacy: The Technologizing of the Word* (New York: Methuen, 1982).

4. Preaching as an immediate response to sudden crisis is, of course, an important responsibility as well. On this, see Joseph R. Jeter, Jr., *Crisis Preaching: Personal and Public* (Nashville, TN: Abingdon, 1998). Homiletician Ronald J. Allen has written two important books that address the need for the systematic address of complex issues: *Preaching the Topical Sermon* (Louisville, KY: Westminster/John Knox Press, 1992), and *The Teaching Sermon* (Nashville, TN: Abingdon Press, 1995). A more recent publication is by Arthur Van Seters, *Preaching and Ethics* (St. Louis: Chalice Press, 2004).

5. Allen Verhey asks the question "What would Jesus do?" (WWJD?) and then addresses "How do we go about figuring out WJWD?" by looking at the varied voices of Scripture and how in moral decision-making they remembered Jesus. See Allen Verhey, *Remembering Jesus: Christian Community, Scripture, and the Moral Life* (Grand Rapids, MI: Eerdmans, 2002), esp. 12–13.

6. Studies in Scripture and ethics have focused on the study of ethics in Scripture and on the nature of Christian ethics as grounded in Scripture and, hence, how Scripture informs moral decision-making. See, for example, Thomas W. Ogletree, *The Use of the Bible in Christian Ethics* (Philadelphia: Fortress, 1983); Allen Verhey, *The Great Reversal: Ethics*

and the New Testament (Grand Rapids, MI: Eerdmans, 1984); Richard B. Hays, *The Moral Vision of the New Testament: Community, Cross, New Creation* (San Francisco: HarperSanFrancisco, 1996); William C. Spohn, *Go and Do Likewise: Jesus and Ethics* (New York: Continuum, 1999); Charles H. Cosgrove, *Appealing to Scripture in Moral Debate* (Grand Rapids, MI: Eerdmans, 2002); and Allen Verhey, *Remembering Jesus.*

7. See Walter Harrelson, *The Ten Commandments and Human Rights* (Philadelphia: Fortress, 1980); Paul Lehmann, *The Decalogue and a Human Future* (Grand Rapids, MI: Eerdmans, 1995); William P. Brown, ed., *The Ten Commandments: The Reciprocity of Faithfulness* (Louisville, KY: Westminster John Knox, 2004); John P. Burgess, *After Baptism: Shaping the Christian Life* (Louisville, KY: Westminster John Knox, 2005).

CHAPTER 6

Mentoring by Mirroring

"THE MEDIUM IS THE MESSAGE." Marshall McCluhan's crisp one-liner reminds us that *what* we communicate is inextricable from *how* we do it.[1] If fostering discernment is the focus of our preaching, it is counterproductive, we have been saying, to set forth "the answer" to a moral quandary. We need to nurture a process, not present a product. That much is obvious, but how to proceed is not. "These are the facts with which we must wrestle; here are moral and theological considerations we must weigh; go figure!" While such reasoning *is* sometimes done in sermons, it will not do. What is the alternative? Sermons that are *mimetic*. By mirroring the process of moral discernment, sermons can mentor a congregation in moral discernment. Moral discernment is mentored by mirroring.

Mentoring by mirroring is the ideal teaching technique when apprentices are learning a "hands-on" skill like carpentry, cooking, playing soccer, or playing a musical instrument.[2] So the challenge in preaching moral discernment is to enact the process itself in a way that the hearers of the Word may participate. Another one-liner, initially addressed to short story writers by Flannery O'Connor, names it nicely: "Show us, don't tell us about it."[3] But easier said than done—especially when the medium is preaching and the skill is moral discernment. This leads us to:

Thesis 6: The rhetorical forms of metaphor, narrative, and argument employed in Scripture by "the preachers of the Bible" are the rhetorical forms necessary to effect preaching for moral discernment.

MIRRORING MORAL DISCERNMENT

All preaching, to be effective, needs to be "engaging" and "evocative," but, as we noted in the last chapter, how those apply in moral discernment preaching is not the same as in funeral or wedding preaching, preaching doxology or intercession. In special occasion sermons (particularly ones dealing with major life transitions), the situation has the "engagement" of listeners built in. "Is there a comforting, clarifying, challenging word for us—here and now?" The question is brought to the sermon by its listeners: they are "leaning in," open to, even eager for an orienting word. In sermons whose center is either praise or petition, what the preacher seeks to evoke can be sharply focused in words and phrases of gratitude or entreaty. Confusion, resistance, or lack of interest may be encountered if the focus of the sermon is a central claim of salvation history (for example, the Ascension of Jesus into heaven, the Trinity, or the nature of God). Nevertheless, by the skillful orchestration of hermeneutical and homiletical listening, preachers can paint "big pictures" that captivate attention and generate response.

When Gospel writers speak of listeners hearing Jesus (or Paul) gladly, and believing his words,[4] they are, we think, bearing witness to the kind of receptivity good preaching effects. Yet subsequent Scriptural passages (in the Gospels, Acts, and the Epistles) also make it clear that to change deeply etched behavior patterns (and patterns of discernment that shape choice and character), more was required for "engaging" and "evoking" than simply setting forth the "kingdom of heaven" parables (Matt 13:31–52, 18:4, 20:1), the "bread of life" discourse (John 6:26–51), Paul's "grace, not law" argument, or his "present your bodies as a living sacrifice" exhortation (Rom 12:1).

Discerning the need for significant shifts in moral direction is difficult because inertia (or resistance) is great. Patterns of behavior are well-established, comfortable, taken-for-granted, almost as involuntary as sleep at the end of the day. So moral discernment requires something akin to being awakened. In fact, to be morally discerning requires openness to reorientation. This happens most often in the midst of hearing other voices, seeing through others' eyes.

These two—the process of moral discernment and openness to change—work together, like love and loving actions, or trust and actions entrusting ourselves to others. Openness may be a state of mind that effects reflective action, but openness is evident and comes about only through reflective actions themselves. Preaching can, therefore, be effective in developing moral discernment only when the sermon mirrors the process of moral discernment. This is what is meant by saying sermons need to be mimetic. The art of preaching must imitate the process of moral discernment, walking through a quandary or crisis, making moves that do not coerce or narrowly define and resolve a moral problem but open a broader sense of what is going on, what is needed, and what are the range of possible, faithful responses. Such sermons must be informed both by a sense of "back and forth" and "step by step." They need to model dialogue and deliberation.

IMAGES, STORIES, AND IDEAS

Again, Wittgenstein's image of language as a toolbox is helpful: words work in different ways. The kind of tools words become depends on their use. Words, phrases, sentences, and paragraphs can be employed as:

- *Images* that convey and evoke sensory awareness: sights, sounds, smells, tastes, touches, feelings.

- *Stories* that articulate a sense of personal identity, and interpersonal history through anecdotes and "slices of life," or through more extended narratives: by depicting settings, characters, and actions that involve conflicts, crises, resolutions, and agendas interrupted or unfinished.

- *Ideas* that express and stimulate efforts to "make sense" of what we see, hear, taste, touch, and smell, by posing questions and concerns, making claims, offering explanations, setting forth cases, raising objections, issuing refutations, and drawing conclusions.[5]

These rhetorical forms are not arbitrary literary conventions. All of us "make sense" of experience by means of an interplay of perception, cognition, and interaction with others. The "language of images" activates our senses; the "language of stories" draws together the unfolding history of our intentions and interactions; the "language of concepts" engages our reflection. Such uses of words are the tools of speech and writing. Images (and metaphors) invite (sometimes impel) us to "Stop and look!" Stories say to us (though indirectly), "Come along and enter in!" We "make sense" of the world we encounter by means of an interweaving of image, story, and idea. "Ideas" (the language of argument) send a different signal: "Pause and consider!" We may lead with one rhetorical form but the others are always in play in the background.

In the task of moral discernment, images are particularly well-suited for naming and evoking moral crises. Image and metaphor are particularly effective for setting forth graphically a sense of where God's people currently are, where (apart from conversion, *metanoia*) they might end up, and how their faith journeys might be redemptively redirected. Those with eyes to see and ears to hear may come to sense the sight and sound of good news when preachers name moral crises clearly with images and metaphors.

Seeking to evoke in his disciples a palpable sense of the oncoming commonwealth of heaven, Matthew's Jesus compares the reign of God both to the serendipitous find of a treasure in a field and to the painstaking search for a priceless pearl (Matt 13:45). Here is metaphorical, imagistic speech—at once disorienting and reorienting.

Narrative, the language of stories, is particularly well-suited for leading listeners into wrestling with moral quandaries. Complex, conflicted choices are not simply concerned with sorting out competing claims of bloodless categories. Running through every moral dilemma is living human drama. Stories are not just entertaining asides, or inspirational climaxes to sprinkle into preaching otherwise comprised of theological analyses and moral assessments. Narratives are at the heart of our lives; they enable us to entertain alternatives, to switch or change stories.

Interdicting a fruitless debate over the meaning of *neighbor* (a moral game his interlocutor can play *ad infinitum*), Luke's Jesus responds (10:30–37) with a "once upon a time" tale of bandits, a victim, religious elites, a social pariah, and an implicated inn keeper. Jesus spins a highly complex socio-religious drama, played out in story form, narrated with elegant simplicity. A world again upended—though by a different genre.

Concepts and arguments are in turn central to leading listeners into reflective analyses concerning the meanings and implications of Christian practices. Choices, we have said, while always particular, are never merely *ad hoc*. They can be appropriately made only in light of broader, deeper patterns of distinctive practice. Neither images nor stories provide sufficient resources for a community to develop its self-delineating practices. For that— whether the concern is immigration reform or the war on terrorism—the orderly setting forth of evidence, the weighing of claim and counterclaim is essential.

John's Jesus uses such a process of reasoning and argument when he engages a woman at the well. Jesus draws her into conversation that moves back and forth around the dynamics of spiritual geography. One more time—racial reorientation, this time by means of argument.

SCRIPTURAL PREACHERS

In terms of preaching for moral discernment, consider the following scriptural texts in the liturgical season of Pentecost (Proper 21 C: Amos 6:1a, 4–7; 1 Tim 6:6–19; and Luke 16:19–31).[6] Each of these texts puts forth the words of a "biblical preacher," addressing his audience on a common topic: the inordinate use of material possessions. Note, however, the different ways in which each preacher works with words:

> Woe to you who are complacent in Zion,
> And to you who feel secure on Mount Samaria!
> You lie on beds inlaid with ivory, and lounge on your couches.
> You dine on choice lambs and fatted calves.
> You strum away on your harps like David
>   and improvise on musical instruments.
> You drink wine by the bowlful and use the finest lotions.
>   but you do not grieve over the ruin of Joseph.
> Therefore you will be among the first to go into exile;
>   your feasting and lounging will end.

Clearly words are working here primarily by way of image and metaphor. Amos is *naming a moral crisis*—calling attention, insistently and dramatically, to "the elephant in the living room" that nobody wants to acknowledge. Amos's mode of engagement is admittedly blatant and shrill, not altogether unlike the terrifying blare of an air raid siren. Yet, the vivid pictures he presents precisely characterize a life of indolent affluence. Sometimes shock treatments are needed.

Less direct than Amos, Luke depicts these words of Jesus:

> There was a rich man who was dressed in purple and fine linen and lived in luxury every day. At his gate was laid a beggar named Lazarus, covered with sores and longing to eat what fell from the rich man's table. Even the dogs came and licked his sores. The time came when the beggar died and angels carried him to Abraham's side. The rich man also died, and was buried. In hell, where he was in torment, he looked up and saw Abraham far away, with Lazarus by his side. So he called to him, "Father Abraham, have pity on me and send Lazarus to dip the tip of his finger in water and cool my tongue, because I am in agony in this fire."
>
> But Abraham replied, "Son, remember that in your lifetime you received good things, while Lazarus received bad things, but now he is comforted here and you are in agony. And besides all this, between us and you a great chasm has

been fixed, so that those who want to go from here to you cannot, nor can anyone cross over from there to us."

He answered, "Then I beg you, father, send Lazarus to my father's house, for I have five brothers. Let him warn them, so that they will not also come to this place of torment."

Abraham replied, "They have Moses and the Prophets; let them listen to them." "No, Father Abraham," he said, "but if someone from the dead goes to them, they will repent." He said to him, "If they do not listen to Moses and the Prophets, they will not be convinced even if someone rises from the dead."

Here, too, imagistic, "picture" language is employed—liberally, in fact. Yet its way of working is primarily by means of an unfolding story line that takes unusual turns *en route* to an ending that its first hearers would have found surprising and deeply unsettling. Less direct, commencing with "once upon a time," Luke places his listeners in the place of overhearing: at a distance that, rather than shutting them out, actually beckons them in. The narrative creates empathy for the plight of two poor men: one in desperate straits on this side of death, one without recourse to resource on death's other side. It is hard not to be torn with pity in both directions, even as one is led to a narrative conclusion as natural (though surprising) as that in the First Letter to Timothy.

Luke's Jesus is, as previously observed, "leading listeners into the rigorous enterprise of wrestling with moral quandaries." It is not enough (suggests Luke's Jesus) to "get the picture," or to "assess in the abstract" (regardless of how important principles and precepts may be). You need to be pulled and pushed, back and forth, amid the competing forces of conflicting claims.

The author of the First Letter to Timothy has a very different way with words than those employed by Amos and Luke:

Godliness with contentment is great gain. For we brought nothing into the world, and we can take nothing out of it. But if we have food and clothing, we will be content with that. People who want to get rich fall into temptation and a trap and into many foolish and harmful desires that plunge men into ruin and destruction. For the love of money is a root of all kinds of evil. Some people, eager for money, have wandered from the faith and pierced themselves with many griefs.

Command those who are rich in this present world not to be arrogant nor to put their hope in wealth, which is so uncertain, but to put their hope in God, who richly provides us with everything for our enjoyment. Command them to do good, to be rich in good deeds, and to be generous and willing to share. In this way they will lay up treasure for themselves as a firm foundation for the coming age, so that they may take hold of the life that is truly life.

Even though some "image" words are sprinkled in here and there, they are employed primarily not as immediate sensory stimuli but as evidence leading toward a conclusion. The author is seeking to foster moral discernment not so much by naming a crisis as by leading his listeners into reflective analysis concerning the meanings and implications of practices (Christian and not-so-Christian). "Weigh and consider!" is the word here. "Assess the long-term implications of short-term gratification!" "Do a cost-benefit analysis of the options," both in terms of character and consequences.

Here is a relatively dispassionate systematic survey, engaging attention by inviting the listener into recognition by means of a fairly straightforward recital of facts easily amenable to empirical verification. The Pauline preacher is leading, clearly; he knows where he is going and wants his listener to follow. But he is incorporating the listener into the process of weighing and considering. By the time he has come to the end of his summarizing assessment, the concluding entreaty to "take hold of life that is truly life" is not so much imposed upon, or even spoken to, but spoken for and with the listener who has become a partner in dialogue in the discernment process.

Dialogue and deliberation are rendered differently in each case—more or less explicit and extensive. Present in each, however, is the clear sense of "back and forth" and "step by step." In each case, the preacher names not merely a value, ideal, or injunction, but an urgent moral crisis. The call is not simply to action, but to reorientation: hearers are offered means by which to make the necessary turning.

CONTEMPORARY EXAMPLES

These scriptural preachers are venerable examples (not to mention canonical), yet they are from long ago and far away. What do such strategies look like in sermons of recognized, contemporary preachers? Once more, a general common sermon theme is used: this time, "God's call to radical hospitality." The preachers are Martin Luther King, Barbara Brown Taylor, and William Sloan Coffin.

The Power of Image

In his widely reproduced sermon "The Drum Major Instinct,"[7] King begins by recapping the story (from Mark 10) of James and John seeking positions next to Jesus. King names their move as "the desire for recognition, for importance," and characterizes it as "the drum major instinct"—an instinct everyone shares with Zebedee's boys.

The drum major instinct begins in a baby's first cry for attention, continues in the competitions of childhood, and goes on undiminished into adult life. King identifies our longings to be praised, to join, and to spend beyond our means as manifestations of the longing to "keep up," "be first."

Having fleshed out his claims in folksy illustrations that elicit rueful chuckles, King makes a sober turn: "There comes a time that the drum major instinct can become destructive." In quick succession he cites instances of "personality distortion": irksome boasting, influence peddling, name-dropping, anti-social (even criminal) behavior—all evidence of our addictive quest for recognition. Unharnessed, the drum major instinct eventually leads us to push others down in order to push ourselves up, generating vicious gossip, and snobbish exclusivism—even (or especially) in the church.

Now King sharpens focus: "the perverted use of the drum major instinct" is the source of "tragic race prejudice." He depicts his encounter with white prison wardens in the Birmingham jail, so economically impoverished that their sense of self-worth is tied to their sense of racial superiority, rendering them oblivious to the forces in American society oppressing black and white alike.

The focus now extends: the drum major instinct drives the struggle for supremacy between nations. "And I am sad to say that the nation in which we live is the supreme culprit. . . . God didn't call America to engage in a senseless, unjust war as the war in Vietnam. And we are criminals in that war. . . . And we won't stop it because of our pride and our arrogance as a nation . . . we have perverted the drum major instinct."

King does not linger in denunciation, however. He returns to the biblical story of Jesus, James, and John. One might expect Jesus to condemn the brothers for their request. But, no, instead he tells them: "You want to be significant. Well, you ought to be. If you're going to be my disciple you must be." Only the priorities need reordering. Greatness need not be renounced—just redefined. "Be first in love . . . first in moral excellence . . . first in generosity." With this definition, "everybody can be great." One only needs "a heart full of grace, a soul generated by love."

King describes the servant ministry of Jesus (identifying him not by name, but actions), then assures us we can all take our places at his right and left hand. In a ringing conclusion of rhetorical cadences depicting acts of service, King writes the servant-epitaph toward which he aspires: "If you want to say that I was a drum major, say that I was a drum major for justice . . . so that we can make of this old world a new world."

No summary can do the sermon justice, of course; it needs to be heard in its entirety. But this sketch reveals the preacher's simple strategy: take an everyday image free of moral, religious, or theological connotations and "change-ring" it strategically. While illustrations abound throughout the sermon, there is little explanation or argument. The success of the sermon depends on the preacher leading listeners through scenes they recognize into a vision of truth on the horizon, a truth that can be ushered into full realization only by communal action. The parade of images is led by that of the "drum major instinct." Voices from many times and places are orchestrated into the dialogue. The dimension of deliberation is effected in a successive "staging" of drum major scenes.

The Trajectory of Story

The story is a second strategy for the preacher who seeks to foster discernment. This time we will let the preacher, Barbara Brown Taylor, speak for herself—both in the telling and in subsequent framing (since that speaks so clearly to what informs her strategy).[8] The initial setting for this presentation was a workshop for preachers. She began as follows:

> Last year, my husband Ed decided that what we needed more than anything was a flock of guinea hens—those unreal-looking salt-and-pepper colored birds with red wattles who make more racket than a pen full of beagles. His first batch of five lasted exactly one day after he let them loose in the yard. We figure that a weasel got them, since all three of the dogs swore that they were innocent. The second batch of five hens also lasted one day, so Ed built a big pen and kept the third batch in it for the better part of a year. The smell was—well, about what you would expect—but the hens survived.
>
> Then a month ago, Ed let them out—and behold, they lived! They quickly took over the five acres around our house, flushing yellow moths from the long grass, and pecking at anything that moved. They also established a pecking order among themselves. Four of them got along fine, but they made life hell for the fifth. They chased her away from the cracked corn Ed pitched to them. They would not let her sit on the fence rail with them. Whatever was wrong with her was invisible to human eyes, but to guinea hen eyes, she was a real leper.
>
> One evening I was down in the garden at dusk, which is when the guinea hens find a low branch to roost on for the night. They picked a young oak that night, right where the clover smell of the pasture meets the deep leaf smell of the woods. One by one, the first four guinea hens took off with a

great beating of wings and huddled on the branch. As each one arrived, the others made room. Finally only the fifth one was left on the ground, but every time she rose to join them they beat her back, screaming at her as they rushed at her with their beaks. After six or seven tries she just stood in the wet grass below them and cried.

The next morning, four guinea hens strutted by my kitchen window. I looked everywhere for the fifth, but she was gone for good. I want to believe that she joined the flock down the road, but I don't think she could have made it that far all by herself. The woods around my house are full of predators—not only weasels but also coyotes and wild dogs. A guinea hen's protection is her flock, only her flock would not have her.

Taylor now moves from immediacy to reflection.

I am not sure how the parable ends, but there it is. I tried to tell it so that you could sense it, but I also tried not to process it too much for you. Instead of telling you how I felt, I tried to show you what made me feel how I felt. Then I left you alone to feel whatever you felt. If it worked, then you thought some things too—about human pecking orders, maybe, or about what happens when we refuse to roost with one another. I tried not to moralize. I just put the dots on the page and let you connect them, so that the conclusion was as much yours as mine.

I learned this straight from Jesus, who knew just when to end a story—often with a question—without wrapping it up too neatly. Did the elder brother ever accept his father's invitation to come to the party, or did he stand out in the yard hating his prodigal brother for the rest of his life? Why was the servant who buried his master's one talent punished for his prudence? Does God really prefer gamblers? What kind of boss pays those who come late to the vineyard the same as those who arrived at daybreak? If that is grace, then it is not fair.

Stories like these carry emotional punch as well as intellectual challenge, but Jesus seemed to know that they would work better if he let his listeners make their own discoveries. . . . People who asked him concrete questions got stories for answers. People who wanted him to settle things for them went away unsettled instead. Sometimes I wonder if he would have lasted as rector of a parish. Somehow I doubt it.

In this sermon segment, moral dialogue and deliberation are embedded in the narrative structure: a framing of life-drama into which listeners are drawn as "over-hearers."

The Engagement of Argument

The language of argument is the third rhetorical strategy. William Sloan Coffin uses this strategy to engage the complex, socially incendiary issues surrounding homosexuality.[9] The reason for using different strategies surely stems in part from differences in personalities and social locations. But another element is in play. Producing a "slide show" of vivid pictures or telling a compelling story to create another sense of the world are not always enough. Making sense by sorting out is sometimes needed. Explanation and argument, tangibly articulated, are necessary.

The preacher begins by listing twenty names—male and female, ancient and modern, artists, athletes, inventors, intellectuals, heads of state—all of whom made "extraordinary contributions to human progress and happiness" and had a homosexual orientation. Citing several daunting social factors—condemnation by Christian ministers, physical and psychological abuse, ostracism by families and churches, and legalized discrimination—Coffin draws a line in the sand: "We have no choice but to bring up the issue . . . American Christians can remain neither indifferent nor indecisive."

Like King, Coffin grounds his advocacy in biblical witness, deftly etching "Saint Peter's struggle to abandon his own fixed certainties, to overcome his own repugnance," and replace them with an open mind and a compassionate heart (Acts 10:1–20). Dwelling on how deeply ingrained in Peter were the Levitical proscription against eating "every swarming thing," Coffin then names the question we face here and now: "whether those of us who were drilled, as was Peter, to think a certain way are as willing as he to risk reexamining what we were taught; and whether we are open to the Holy Spirit's leading, in our own time, toward a fresh realization that 'God shows no partiality.' "

Borrowing a set of distinctions from a Christian ethicist,[10] Coffin proceeds to analyze four possible stances toward homosexuality: rejecting-punitive (homosexuality is sinfulness), rejecting-nonpunitive (homosexuality is sickness), conditional acceptance (homosexuality, while permissible, is not ideal), and unconditional acceptance (homosexuality is but one of many manifestations of difference in the human family).

Primary energy is given to critical analysis of the first option:

- The Levitical code (cited as biblical justification for proscribing homosexual behavior) concerned not matters of moral precept but ritual purity (e.g., eating pork, misusing incense).

- Israel's worship deliberately repudiated local fertility cult practices of employing ritual prostitutes—male and female. At issue: idolatry, not homosexuality.

- In the ancient Middle East, forced anal rape was used to humiliate captured foes. The particular focus of prohibition: "dishonoring a fellow human being."

- The prohibition may have involved a belief that male sperm was the life carrier (and procreation was essential for a tiny nation surrounded by large hostile ones).

- Homosexual orientation, as such, is never addressed in Scripture.

- The primary prophetic condemnations of Sodom and Gomorrah address injustice to the socially marginalized, and failure in hospitality. ("How ironic that because of a mistaken understanding of the crime of Sodom and Gomorrah, Christians should be repeating the real crime every day against homosexuals!")

- In conclusion: "The problem is not how to reconcile homosexuality with scriptural passages that appear to condemn it, but rather how to reconcile the rejection and punishment of homosexuality with the love of Christ. I do not think it can be done."

The "rejecting-nonpunitive" approach (not sinful, but sick) Coffin engages more succinctly. The testimony of those who affirm they did not chose their sexual orientation is supported by scientific research. "If gays can be as loving as straights, then why is homosexual love contrary to human nature?" Coffin continues, "Should a relationship not be judged by its inner worth rather than by its outward appearance?"

Coffin confesses that he has tended toward the alternative of conditional acceptance (properly protected, legally, but less than ideal). But citing the history of Jewish-Christian relations, race relations, and relations between men and women, he asks: "Can you champion equality while nourishing the theological roots that make for inequality?" Then he presses the point further: by refusing to support homosexual relationships, straights bear as much responsibility for unstable homosexual relationships as those whites who made sure there would be no reward for the economic diligence of blacks whom they branded as "shiftless."

Coffin concludes: "So enough of these fixed certainties. If what we think is right and wrong still further divides the human family, there must be something wrong with what we think is right. . . . Peter widened his horizons; let's not narrow ours. . . . Let's listen, learn, let's read and pray—none of this is easy—until with Peter's conviction we can make a similar confession: 'Truly I perceive that God shows no partiality, but in every sexual orientation any one who fears him and does what is right is acceptable to him.'"

The approach Coffin takes is the classic argument strategy of *via negativa*—not this, that, or the other alternatives (plausible though they sound, "natural" though they seem), because the reasons offered in defense of each do not stand up to scrutiny. The last remaining, and most challenging, alternative, therefore (which can, upon examination, be better supported) is the one best commending itself to choice and action. Dialogue and deliberation are woven through this sermon from beginning to end. Though many resources are employed by the preacher, he is essentially supplying information for an unfolding conversation with the understanding of listeners, providing them with the materials by means of which listeners can (with the Spirit's help) convince themselves.

—⌒—

With Amos, Luke, the "Paul" who wrote 1 Timothy—and then again with King, Taylor, and Coffin—we have heard three strategic ways of seeking to effect moral discernment in the hearers of the Word.

- Amos and King effect moral discernment primarily through deploying images that name a moral crisis—providing lenses, windows, icons for vividly identifying (without superficially rendering) choices that, however difficult and demanding, will be made—by quasi-conscious avoidance, if not by deliberate decision.

- Luke and Taylor plot their narratives of communal discernment by means of straightforward storytelling, sweeping us into moral quandary-wrestling immediately, rather than by means of metaphors or concepts. Decision-making is not simply a matter of "getting the picture" or of "weighing the options." Quandaries cannot be addressed from a distance. We bring our own stories to the struggle; no, we extend our own stories in the drama of decision-making. While everyone has his or her "own story," community is created by the discovery of points of deep resonance in our respective "story lines." In the midst of moral wrestling, parables sometimes do what pictures and points cannot alone achieve.

- "Paul" and Coffin effect moral discernment through ideas arranged in argument, attempting to evoke reflective analysis concerning the meanings and implications of Christian practices. Behind "what should we do?" is "why should we do it?" Or, often more immediately: "Why should we change directions from what is current, comfortable, 'natural'"? The demand to "set forth your case" is not a dodge. Deliberation is a necessary prelude to responsible action. Well-considered, well-presented arguments are an essential response to "fair questions."

Our question has been, "How can pulpit proclamation foster moral formation and discernment?" Where have we come thus far?

We have acknowledged some formidable challenges to such a calling: factors inherent in moral judgment, conditions characteristic of contemporary culture, and issues particular to communities of faith (chapter 1). To engage these challenges, we have proposed:

- Appropriating the Scriptures as open-ended explorations of God's continuing action in the world and in dialogue with our experience (chapter 2, thesis 1).

- Employing Christian practices as interpretive lenses for moral analysis in situations of crisis and quandary (chapters 3 and 4).

- Using homiletical strategies as catalysts for engaging sustained congregational reflection on issues of moral significance (chapters 5 and 6).

Along the way we have offered examples of how these various elements can be brought fruitfully into play in the process of preaching.

In what follows we want to offer more illustrations, with primary focus on two other proposals introduced in chapter 2: to interplay quandary and practice (thesis 3), and to access narratives of communal discernment implicit in the Epistles (thesis 2). Having now discussed both practice lenses and homiletical strategies, we are able to consider more concretely what such preaching might sound like.

Notes

1. Marshall McLuhan, Quentin Fiore, and Jerome Agel, *The Medium is the Massage* (New York: Bantam, 1967). While the phrase for which he has become famous is as noted above, McLuhan thought "massage" (a publisher's error) was appropriate and the title remained.

2. Donald A. Schoen, *The Reflective Practitioner* (New York: Basic Books, 1982). In terms of educating clergy, see Charles R. Foster, Lisa E. Dahill, Lawrence A. Golemon, and Barbara Wang Tolentino, *Educating Clergy: Teaching Practices and Pastoral Imagination* (San Francisco: Jossey-Bass, 2006).

3. See Flannery O'Connor, *The Habit of Being: Letters of Flannery O'Connor*, ed. Sally Fitzgerald (New York: Farrar, Strauss & Giroux, 1979).

4. See, for instance, Matthew 7:28–29; Mark 1:21–28; John 2:22–24; John 10:41–42; Acts 13:47–49; 17:10–11; 18:8.

5. See David J. Schlafer, *Playing with Fire: Preaching Work as Kindling Art* (Boston: Cowley Publications, 2004).

6. The Scripture quotations that follow are taken from The New International Version of the Bible.

7. Martin Luther King, "The Drum Major Instinct," in *A Testament of Hope: The Essential Writings of Martin Luther King, Jr.*, ed. James M. Washington (San Francisco: Harper, 1986), 259–67.

8. This material is taken from a lecture presented by Barbara Brown Taylor to participants in the Preaching Excellence Program, and has been reprinted in *Preaching Through the Year of Matthew: Sermons that Work X*, ed. Roger Alling and David J. Schlafer (Harrisburg, PA: Morehouse Publishing, 2001), ix–xi.

9. See O. C. Edwards, Jr., *A History of Preaching* (Nashville, TN: Abingdon, 2004), 739–41; the text of the sermon is included in the accompanying CD-ROM. The text may be also found in Henry Sloan Coffin, *The Courage to Love* (San Francisco: Harper, 1982), 39–47.

10. James B. Nelson, "Homosexuality," in *The Westminster Dictionary of Christian Ethics*, ed. James F. Childress and John Macquarrie (Philadelphia: Westminster, 1986), 271–73.

CHAPTER 7

Quandary and Practice

WE HAVE BEEN UNFOLDING LAYER BY LAYER what is entailed in preaching moral discernment. In the sermon "Is It Lawful for a Christian to Gamble?" we listened to a preacher who employs a story as an open-ended narrative in conversation (literally) with important unfinished business and unanswered questions about an open-ended narrative in one community's experience. This is the first fundamental feature of preaching moral discernment, though bringing Jesus into a noisy gambling hall is by no means the only way of going about it. (Note the differing but analogous strategy at work in the sermon reprinted in chapter 1, where the preacher seeks to engage his congregation with questions of sexual morality.)

"Give therefore to the emperor the things that are the emperor's, and to God the things that are God's"—that saying of Jesus is often handled homiletically as a conversation-squelching *ipse dixit*. ("Now hear *this*!") But in this sermon Jesus' words function as a moral focus rather than a moral fix. They open up communal reflection rather than shutting it down. (Note the parallel, again, in the earlier sermon dealing with Jesus' words in Luke's Gospel about neglecting "justice and the love of God.").

Employing practices as lenses is a second basic feature in preaching toward moral discernment. "Shock Therapy" (presented at the end of chapter 4) is not a sermon about how reconciliation, householding, hospitality, or citizenship can enable those faced with hard questions to rise above the quandary. Rather these Christian practices bring into focus the factors on which fruitful dialogue regarding this crisis need to turn.

None of the three sermons we have considered dwells primarily on "salvation history." Neither do they attempt to solve the moral quandary; rather, each sets the moral issue in the context of the Gospel imperatives, broadly understood.

A third fundamental feature in preaching toward moral discernment is mimesis: mentoring the process of moral discernment, "making sense" by mirroring it through an interplay of tension and *telos* that is deployed through rhetorical strategies of image, story, and argument. It is this interplay that animates and engages listeners. The three sermons we have considered develop the tension we confront in the quandary we face in order to explore the understanding of Christian faith for our lives. They do this by variously drawing upon biblical images, stories, and arguments. The first sermon poses the question by illustrating the discrepancy between how homosexuality is addressed in the military and in the church and poses the seemingly anachronistic words of Luke's Jesus with striking, fresh relevance. The "casino" sermon moves rhetorically between narrative and image, with an interspersing of analytical commentary. The "shock therapy" sermon uses question-posing images and brief narrative scenes to probe an argument about hospitality and community. Fundamentally these sermons seek to mentor the process of moral discernment, as do the sermons by King, Taylor, and Coffin summarized and/or excerpted in chapter 6.

Now, while continuing to illustrate these features, we turn to highlight how quandaries and practices mutually inform each other in preaching toward moral discernment.

"Forgiveness and reconciliation"—what relevance has this Christian practice in the wake of 9/11? The following sermon was requested for a service marking the end of a two-week marathon of services at a parish near where one airplane hit the Pentagon site in Washington, D.C. While the Scriptures chosen were ones appointed for the Burial of the Dead, and the liturgical context was a celebration of the Eucharist, no other elements of the funeral liturgy were used. Since many in attendance were of other faiths (or no faith), the sermon needed to be especially hospitable.

Homiletical commentary will be interspersed throughout the first sermon, followed by specific observations on the "back and forth" between the practice lens of "forgiveness and reconciliation" and the moral quandary created by the crisis.

WHAT ARE WE GOING TO DO NOW?[1]
Isaiah 61:1–6; Psalm 27; Revelation 21:1–7; Matthew 5:1–16

Oh my God! What are we going to do now? That is the question we instinctively ask when all of a sudden our world blows apart. Oh my God! What are we going to do now?

The first time we ask the question—as fireballs flare, and towers collapse—the answer is spontaneous, thoughtless, wordless. Our bodies do the talking—hearts pound, faces freeze, muscles jerk. We do not pause to consider the options—the answer is automatic: What are we going to do now? Duck and run! Get out of here!

The sermon commences by acknowledging the devastating images and feelings of the moment, and proceeds to direct those experiences to progressively deeper levels.

But there is more to this question than a first response can give. It comes again, a second time: What are we going to do now? And maybe because it's our job, what we get paid to do, but more likely because it springs from an instinct as deep as self-protection, a second answer comes to the second asking: What are we going to do now? Reach out and help!

Not much calculation in this response either. "It'll look great on my resume." "My mother will be so proud." "Tough job, but good pay." No—none of the above. Rather, the raw imperative of pure human freedom: "They're in danger; I gotta go. I must do something—whatever I can—whatever it takes!"

Natural human wellsprings of the practice of hospitality are acknowledged and honored.

But the question doesn't go away with Answer Number Two. Indeed, the very answer offered in heroic rescue action rekindles the question with greater force: "Limited success, dwindling hope, lives lost, loves torn": What are we going to do now?

And another answer makes its way into our asking space, still spontaneous, but now more measured: "Mourn and weep." And so we have done, since unforgettable Tuesday—wells of tears brimming, floods of tears falling from our eyes—eyes of all ages, all races, all religions (and no religion). Tears of women, unashamed tears from males, for a change. Tears of grandfathers, aunts, children, neighbors—tears of citizens from many nations. Every tear appropriate—no tear wasted.

Has anyone ever told you: "That's nothing to cry over!" "There, there—don't cry." Or, "You stop that crying, right this minute!"? Well, maybe they have at some time or another. But I'll bet they haven't said such things to you in the last few days. Oh My God! What are we going to do now? Mourn and weep.

Mourn and weep—but once again, the answer regenerates the question. So many people mourning and weeping. What are we going to do now? As the question goes deeper, a deeper answer comes as well. Hug and hold. Stricken though you are, you can embrace the stricken. You don't have to flash a "no scars" badge. Your own scars credential you for hugging and holding the wounded and weeping.

The source of hospitality is more specifically named as "compassion."

But after that—then what? What are we going to do now? A cascade of options spills across the mental screen. Storm and rage! Strike back! Hunker down! Put it behind you and just get on. So many options, none without reason, not all contradictory— but not all compatible. And this may be why we have witnessed and shared still another dimension of "going and doing" in recent days—stopping what we're doing and sitting still. Not the "sitting still" of paralyzed fear, dazed stupor, or sheer denial, but a stopping and sitting to honor and treasure rich resources no violent attack can ever destroy—good deeds done, lives of grace lived—unrepentant lanterns, shining in a dark world.

But "stopping and sitting still" has meant something else for us, I think: a deliberate determination to pause and reflect, before moving on. Do you hear it coming—the question again: What are we going to do now? It is a time to sit and be still, so that the question can work its way down to who we deeply are, and who we wish to become.

The dialogical dimension, the "back and forth" is directly incorporated into the sermon plot in a deliberate move to initiate the process of "mentoring by mirroring." The sermon shapes the critically important "breathing space" Rowan Williams calls for. The necessity of a discernment process is described without being explicitly enjoined.

We are told we need closure, so we can begin to put our lives back together and move forward. In some ways, surely, we do need such closure. But there are significant respects in which closure on "the recent tragic events" (as they are already being tagged) is as inappropriate as it is impossible. Even if a return to business as usual were an available option—which, of course, it is not—few of us would want to go there. Too much has been de-centered, too much is up for grabs, too much is at stake. What are we going to do now?

Again "back and forth" tensions are both acknowledged and encouraged. The need for spiritual resources to serve as "practice lenses" can now be suggested.

But how can we explore the abyss of that question, if all we have to listen to are the sounds of our own voices, reverberating in the echo chambers of our own minds? If all we have to draw upon are words pouring forth from the media—shrill, strident words demanding our hearing? Perhaps there are other voices who might be invited to join us in the questioning journey. Voices of those, themselves, pushed beyond the breaking point of senseless suffering, inflicted by violence, terrorism, cruelty. Voices of those we call people of faith. Voices that might not tell us just what we wanted to hear. But voices that might help us hear what we need to do.

"Speak to us, elder sisters and brothers! We have not been, most of us, in a place like this before. Speak to us—we have need of your company—need of your wisdom."

And listening, as we have today, to the voices of a song writer, a poet-prophet, a subversive teacher, and a wide-eyed visionary, here are things we do *not* hear: an executive order—"Now Hear This!" (to which the answer can only be: "Yes sir; whatever you say, sir!"). This is also what we do not hear: empty, pious platitudes—"Just trust God; it's gonna be all right." No—what we hear are strange words—words quiet and wild.

Misunderstandings (and misappropriations) of "the Word of the Lord" are named and set aside, so that iconic elements in open-ended narratives both of salvation and discernment can be heard as fresh, live, and relevant for dealing with the discernment question: "What are we going to do now?"

"The LORD is my light and my salvation; whom then shall I fear? . . . One thing I asked of the LORD...to live in the house of the LORD all the days of my life." Not an escape from chaos, a cozy cave in which to ride out the storm, but "the house of the Lord"—a dwelling place, a living space, an energy center for a journey through hell.

Lines from Psalm 27 are interpreted and employed as practice lenses of prayer and worship, and householding.

"Show me your way, O Lord," the songwriter sings. "Because I do have enemies; Oh God, lead me on a level path."

Where will that level path lead us? Another voice, the voice of a poet-prophet offers an answer: the level path will lead us "to bring good news to the oppressed, to bind up the broken-hearted, to proclaim liberty to captives"—not only to prison inmates, but also to long-time victims of economic and political oppression. God's "level path" will lead us, the poet-prophet suggests, to counter works of terror with a curious vengeance—the proclamation of God's Radical Peace. To comfort mourners, to rebuild ruined cities—-not just to rebuild towers from rubble; but to dig through, as Isaiah says: the devastation of many generations that fires acts of terrorism and violence.

The words of Isaiah are employed as lenses of hospitality and citizenship, brought to bear as alternative approaches to violence brandished in service of self-defense or retribution.

Hold it! Time out! We are in no position to do that!

Once again, realistic resistance is given sermon space—and directly answered with a fresh glossing of familiar phrases from the Sermon on the Mount.

"Indeed you are," cuts in the voice of the subversive-teacher. Blessed are the poor in spirit, those who mourn. Blessed are the meek (those who don't have arrogant answers at the tips of their tongues). Blessed are those who want righteous justice (fair distribution, not quick retribution). Blessed are those who want righteousness so badly they can all but taste it. Those who long for justice so deeply, it feels like the pangs of a stomach that hasn't eaten for days, like a dehydrated body, desperate for water.

"Blessed are those who show mercy—regardless. Blessed are those who work for peace—whatever it costs. Blessed—NOT 'blessed,' the way the President's Press Secretary used the word recently—'the citizens of our country have a blessed life'— (which is not, any more, true in quite the way it was when he said it!); but blessed are we. You and I are in the best possible place, the most strategic position to realize the Reign of God—a Commonwealth more real than anything else around."

The contrast between the values of empire and those of God's In-breaking Commonwealth are sharply juxtaposed.

And then, if that's not overload enough, here comes the word that is really wild, prefaced by a sight too good not to be true. A new heaven and new earth—free from horror and carnage, a new city coming down from God—coming down to connect with the reaching-up work of mourners, mercy messengers, peacemakers. A new city, proving once and for all that heaven has nothing to do with "pie in the sky by and by."

Narratives of salvation history and communal discernment are named as complementary, with an implicit invitation to confront the human carnage and moral outrage of terrorist attacks with forgiveness and hospitality.

But wait—that isn't all—the word comes again: "See—the home of God is among mortals." See—God dwells among human beings. God will be with them, as they belong to God. And—oh look—do you see that? God wiping every tear, one by one, from every weeping human eye!

Let's take a deep breath, so we can take this in. Wiping tears—not saying, "Stop that crying!" But wiping tears from eyes blinded by pain, and grief, and rage. Wiping and wiping—tear after tear—for as long as it takes, for as many who will, so that all can turn with fresh eyes and behold God's new city.

"See, I am making all things new." That's what God says, as God wipes away tears. That is a closure worth having! And that is the only closure with a chance in the world, because it is a closure that opens toward utterly new life.

A vision of God's action, shaped by prayer and worship, sets a context for forgiveness and reconciliation, householding and hospitality, with radical implications for what it means to be a citizen. It is developed, of course, from the biblical image.

Impractical? It all depends how you define the word. Frankly, in these voices, I hear a clear sense of direction. A marching order I can salute—freely and gladly—with all that I am and all that I do. What I am hearing is this: when our fingers touch the tears of inconsolable suffering, then our fingers are in touch with the finger of God. And if the only way our fingers find to dry the tears of some is to do what makes others weep—well, it is just possible that what we will hear is a firm, quiet voice saying: "See here! I am busy drying tears! It is not necessary to bring tears in order to dry tears. On this one, either you are with me or you are not."

At its very end, the sermon turns to direct but implicit critique of a political orientation that, because incompatible with Christian practice, cannot legitimately claim to be following the One born "in the beauty of the lilies," whose "truth is marching on."

"Oh my God! What are we going to do now?"
"O dear God! Please help us do what we need to do now!"

The question with which the sermon opens is left open, having been progressively reframed.

Christian practices, not named as abstract nouns, but depicted as active verbs, serve as the means of helping listeners make sense of the tragedy. Not by explaining or justifying the attacks, but in discerning courses of action that can address them through redemptive work. Furthermore, the practice lenses are themselves given fresh meaning as they are brought into a "back and forth" with crises and quandaries catalyzed by 9/11. Reconciliation and hospitality, for instance, are pushed to the limit in terms of the behavior patterns they suggest, not just in response to the attacks, but in light of them, in response to grievances that fester and needs that call from the fringes of everyday consciousness.

The sermon does not tell listeners precisely how to respond. (How could it, so soon after such a trauma?) It does, however, set a context for a continuing, critically important conversation (a fact made fairly obvious by ensuing decisions and subsequent events that were essentially uninformed by such a conversation). But the immediacy of unexpected disaster does not necessarily preclude more pointed pulpit speech.

Consider now the following, preached exactly four years after 9/11, and immediately after the other crisis that served as a springboard for this volume: the aftermath of Hurricane Katrina. It will be presented without interruption, followed by a more systematic commentary.

SEVENTY TIMES SEVEN[2]
Matthew 18:21–35

"Seven times?" asks Peter. Peter knows the code of the day: the eye for an eye, the tooth for a tooth, the social contract of the Hebrew culture that called for an equal distribution of justice. He knows that Jesus is instructing the new community in how to be the church, and he wants to prove that he gets it. He's showing off. Eager-beaver Peter says he is ready to forgive a wrong not just once, but seven times over!

Is Jesus impressed? Is seven times enough? No. He gives a new number, seventy times seven, a symbolic number, a number beyond imagining. You need to forgive a gazillion times, Jesus says, again and again and again.

Oh-oh. Is this another one of those camel-through-the-needle's eye moral standards, another turn-the-other-cheek, go-the-extra-mile? Is seventy times seven just another recipe for guilt? What about those times it's hard to cough up even a half-hearted "I forgive you"? This might mean I have to change!

There *is* a call to change in Jesus' call for forgiveness. But this is not so much a command as a *promise*. In calling for a climate of forgiveness, Jesus offers a whole new social contract, a community based on living in the freedom of God's forgiveness. He called it the kingdom of heaven, remember? He went around saying, "Repent, change your ways, the kingdom of heaven is here."

Jesus' call for change, for this new social contract, this new kingdom, stood in sharp contrast to the way of the Roman Empire. It stood in sharp contrast to the temple religion that joined in mute collaboration with the Roman Empire to maintain the status quo, a status quo established in Israel some ten centuries earlier, a status quo that echoed the dynasties of the Pharaohs. In each Empire, from the Pharaohs to the Babylonians to the Greeks to the Romans, a small group of economic elites controlled the huge peasant underclass. And a whole system of social and political and religious codes kept the structure in place. But then along comes Jesus, making trouble. He says that way is not right. God cares about the way the world is organized, and God's way is different.

With this call to forgiveness, Jesus offers a way of life characterized not by duplicity and intrigue, but by open, honest, plain speech. He describes the way of God, a way of forgiveness, a way of relating based on trust, integrity, mutual respect, and truth. Because we can't get to forgiveness if we can't first name the truth.

Think about what it is to be lied to. When all of a sudden, or with a slow, steady realization, you see that you have been betrayed. We know the muscle of a lie, how a lie keeps the liar in a position of knowing, a position of power over the other. We know what it feels like when someone withholds the whole truth, or changes a story to control a situation. We know the confusion, the betrayal. There is nothing like being on the receiving end of a lie to make us understand the reason that the Ninth Commandment was important to those Hebrews of the Exodus. A lie cripples our ability to trust. A lie rips apart the fabric of a community.

So, to build community, we are to forgive seventy times seven. The flip side of that, we could say, seventy times seven, we are to tell the truth. The two go hand in hand. We cannot forgive until we acknowledge that something is amiss. We cannot forgive until we name the wrong. Without that truth-telling, that naming of what's real and not illusion, we can't begin to forgive. And then, when reality is exposed, when the truth is told, and the false images lie shattered on the floor like so many fragments of a cheap hand mirror—only then is the time for building at hand.

Today is such a time, a time for building in the wake of hurricane Katrina, a time for building on the anniversary of 9/11. But we are a little out of practice with the tools needed for building the kind of community that Jesus talked about. We are out of practice, because truth-telling and forgiveness are at a premium in our world, as they were in Peter's. Peter needed the practice because he operated so often under a set of illusions about his own good intentions. But when push came to shove, Peter was just as self-protective, cowardly, equivocating, just as human as I am, or you are.

The good news here is that Jesus' interest in forgiveness was not limited to my private virtue or yours. Jesus' focus was always on the common good. He gave his teaching and preaching and his whole life for a new way of living for all, a way of life centered on a God of forgiveness and freedom, a radical new way that was not the way of commerce or monarchy or the military or even religion. This way of Jesus, where truth speaks to power, where forgiveness flourishes, where communities thrive, where caring for the least among us is our hallmark—well the world hadn't seen anything like that. It didn't match anything at hand. And it still doesn't.

Look at our time, this new twenty-first century American Empire of ours. Where is truth today? What is truth? Pilate could ask again. Four years after the national shock of 9/11, the crashing of those passenger jets into the twin towers, the Pentagon, and a Pennsylvania farm field, we find ourselves in a setting where appearances do not match reality.

Four years ago, as a nation, we did not dwell long on the horror of that day, on all that we lost: the loss of life, the loss of our illusion of safety, the loss of any innocence we had left. We did not examine our role in the family of nations, we did not examine the impact of our support of Israel on the Arab world. We did not examine the roots of terrorism. We—all of us, private citizens, our press corps, our elected officials in both parties—we all failed to examine why this happened, why we ignored the signs of impending attack.

We did not question our leaders—to do so was unpatriotic. We did not grieve our losses long, but salved our grief with hero-stories, preferring to focus on the brave men and women who went into the rubble again and again to recover anyone they could. They were heroes, to be sure, true heroes; but focus on them distracted us from the full truth of this overwhelming tragedy. The heroes helped us feel good about ourselves again, and we needed something to feel good about to take our minds off the evil that had invaded our lives. So we jumped from shock and grief to run the flag back up to full mast within a month, and to chart a sure and steady course toward war, a war we were told was about weapons of mass destruction, or about some link between Osama and Iraq, a war to nip terrorism in its bud, a war where the first casualty was truth.

We live in a time that looks like an Aldous Huxley or George Orwell novel, where one thing is said, another meant. We all participate. We hear about Homeland Security and then, in the wake of Hurricane Katrina, see that homeland security has left us shamefully insecure and ill-prepared: Our National Guard is not able to be at the ready; they are the overextended farm team for the war in Iraq. We have seen horrific images of death and despair; we have seen truth splashed across our TV screens as never before. We have seen the news, we are hearing the voices from the left and from the right, about the dismantling of FEMA in the name of Homeland Security, we are hearing serious accusations that some would dismiss as a "blame game."

And I bet you don't want to hear them from this pulpit, especially on this glorious Sunday when we are returning for another program year, when we are bringing our children to learn how to be people of faith, how to be Christians in this world. It is so much more uplifting to focus on our newest stories of heroism, the good news of light in the midst of this dark storm. There are such stories, to be sure; and we have those heroes, thank God. We need stories of courage and hope, as desperate victims need a hero's rescue. I wish I could preach a sermon filled with such hopeful stories. It might help me feel less outrage; it might make me feel better.

But the challenge to me, as a Christian, to us, as moral people, is not to try to feel good again. The challenge is to tell the truth. We are here to teach our children, to practice a kind of speech uncommon in the parlance of our day. We must learn to tell the truth, and to ask for it. We must ask the hard questions because we believe in Jesus' promise of another way to live, another way to organize the world.

I don't mean that our job is to point fingers about the debacle in the Gulf states. We can point fingers all over the place about lack of preparedness, cuts in funding to FEMA, the Army Corps of Engineers, or levee repair, about shortages in our National Guard, poor local, regional, and national governance, and on and on. We can see the gaps between public pronouncements and the actual emergency responses.

But the gleaming underbelly that we have seen exposed, the truth to tell here, is about our old and evil institution: racism and its twin sister poverty. Not only did we leave the poor and elderly and sick behind in the event of this hurricane, we have been leaving them behind for decades and generations. We live, in this richest nation in the world, with a permanent underclass. We allow one half of the children of Louisiana and Mississippi to live below the poverty line, and we have established that line at $18,000 for a family of four. We give these children woefully equipped schools. We allow their neighborhoods to be the hunting grounds of the most desperate of these children—the uneducated, unemployed young men who have traded in hope for a handgun. And with each delicious tax cut served up by Congress, another social service—from police to schools to public health—shrinks its paltry efforts in these ravaged city streets.

And even as our Congress sends $62 billion in aid to the Gulf states—a recognition that government comes in handy once in awhile!—our President has suspended the Davis-Bacon Act, allowing federal contractors to pay less than a prevailing wage to workers on re-construction projects. So now the workers who will be rebuilding the Gulf region, as they also try to rebuild their homes and family livelihoods, these construction workers can be paid less than the prevailing local wage of $9 an hour. The cycle of poverty spins on.

We allow that. We accept that. We participate in that. Our mutual funds will see a bump up from this. That is our shame, our collective shame. It does not belong to one political party. The underbelly of poverty and racism in our country is a profound moral challenge, to me and to you, to any one of us who say we are the followers of the One who said, "Blessed are the poor."

It is our vocation, our calling, as Christians, to tell the truth. To name reality for what it is, to question what seems to be not right, from the smallest equivocation in a staff meeting to the damaging withholding of truth in a friendship to the corrosive pattern of lying that keeps a black African-American underclass at the bottom of our economic pyramid. We are to tell the truth, practice it, seventy times seven, again and again and again.

Some of our leaders have been calling for truth. The clearest, boldest call I have heard comes from one of our modern-day saints, Rabbi Michael Lerner, editor of *Tikkun* magazine. Lerner says we are too timid if we critique only the emergency response. He says we can "no longer ignore the underlying class and race issues that systematically place the poorest and most vulnerable at highest risk." The rabbi has a dream. He has issued a call for a new Marshall Plan to rebuild New Orleans, and beyond that, to provide upgraded housing for the poor of all of America's inner cities, to upgrade the social support infrastructure of those cities. The cost would be high: $80 billion a year, comparable to the latest supplemental funding for the war in Iraq. If we did this for five years, he said, "we would have taken an important step toward our moral obligation as a society and would be putting meaning behind the biblical injunctions to care for the poor and the powerless."

It's a dream. But sometimes, we need someone who dares to say, "I have a dream." Rabbi Michael Lerner, like Martin Luther King, Jr., like our rabbi Jesus, asks us to dare to look at the truth, to speak truth, to speak truth to power. Not easy, not for Peter, not for me. Because it begins with change. The kingdom of heaven, Jesus said, is here. And another word for change is repent. Repent. Once, seven times, seventy times seven. Because the kingdom of heaven begins now.

Several homiletical observations:

- While the social commentary here is much more directed and extensive than in the previous sermon, the critique does not become a politically partisan "blame game," but rather a searching descriptive analysis of powerful, interconnected, and hidden unconscious social factors constituting the crisis that the storm only brought to light.

- Even though the call to action is more specifically focused than in the previous sermon, there remains room for the continuing process of communal discernment. The sermon sets the stage for moral conversation; it seeks to open conversation.

- A quick survey of the principles proposed in chapter 5 shows that this sermon embodies every one. There is tension and *telos* played out in terms of what God is calling in the midst of crisis and quandaries. The sermon begins with and is grounded in the discernment offered in Scripture as it is equally informed by a vision of the practices of the Christian life. Throughout it emphasizes corporate accountability and response.

- While the previous sermon is primarily in the mode of Amos and King, this one is much more in the mode of argument, as were "Paul" and Coffin (chapter 6).

- It is evident that the Christian practice lenses of forgiveness, householding, hospitality, and citizenship are employed throughout to interpret recent events and long-entrenched social patterns. Less overtly, but no less definitely, "prayer and worship" are in play as well.

- The necessary truth-telling integral to forgiveness (discussed in chapter 3) receives extensive treatment. More important, in the back and forth between a familiar biblical text on forgiveness, and the hard truths Hurricane Katrina requires us to face, a deepened understanding is posed regarding the relationship between truth telling and forgiving than that which is conventionally associated with Jesus' command to Peter.

TWO SERMON SEGMENTS CENTERED ON OLD TESTAMENT TEXTS

Using Hurricane Katrina once again, here are excerpts from a sermon preached several months after the storm by a parish priest in New Orleans. This time, however, the primary practice lenses are "Prayer and Worship," and "Reverence for Creation." The biblical point of entry appears initially as most unlikely—the Genesis account of the sacrifice of Isaac (Gen 22:1–19).

—◦—

SACRIFICES TO MOLECH[3]

No one can hear the breathtaking story of Abraham and Isaac without being moved. Meaning in this story can never be exhausted; there is always more to fathom—about God, about Abraham, and about ourselves.

In Abraham's time, sacrificing children seems to have been a common practice, not to Yahweh, our God, but to Molech, a hungry idol that demanded to be appeased or terrible consequences might follow. The Abraham and Isaac story makes it very clear that Yahweh is NOT Molech, or a god like Molech, but clearly Molech worship was at issue. We hear these ancient stories and dismiss them as primitive, not very connected to us, but then one day, not long ago, I wondered.

I was driving out to our house on the lakefront when that huge mound of stuff taken out of everyone's houses was piled up between West End Boulevard and Pontchartrain. Sofas, tables, bicycles, bed frames, TVs, toys: everything imaginable was in that heap. I thought about Gehenna, the garbage dump outside Jerusalem, a place of destruction and death traditionally associated with Molech.

No, we don't sacrifice children to Molech, not directly, but a new awareness came over me—that in not paying far more attention to the destruction of our valuable wetlands, in not tending to the levees properly, we have sacrificed the life many of our children might have enjoyed by growing up here.

We will pass on to them an environment we have not only allowed to deteriorate, but have, in many instances, sacrificed to the gods of profit from oil production through the digging of canals and through the development of former wetlands as real estate.

What our children may inherit from us is an uninhabitable mess, a mess of our doing, or to put it another way, our undoing of God's creation.

But, most of all, we have failed to understand the neglect and sacrifice of our precious wetlands as a spiritual question. Our collective yielding to material interests is not simply an economic issue but has deep spiritual dimensions. It is God's earth, God's creation. Exploitation of the environment is a sin. God intends for us to use and to protect nature, not to destroy it.

There is hope. Our God is not Molech but Yahweh, the God of salvation. We can turn back to God and we can adopt better ways. With God's help, we can turn things around, even our-selves. As spiritually driven people, it is our responsibility to raise the tough environmental questions with every person running for public office. As God's children ourselves, we need to ensure that God's gift of this lovely world is there for our children to enjoy and to protect. This is no small order; it means confronting greed and the powers that would destroy God's creation for their own benefit.

Like Abraham, this is a test of our faith. Do we understand that we are God's first and that we only secondarily belong to ourselves? Do we have the inner resources to make a better world for our children?

Clearly, the Abraham story, and our responsibility for environmental stewardship, are each seen in fresh perspective when interpreted through the lens of the other. A worship ritual, ancient and alien, is seen in new light, both in its own context, and in its sobering interpretive implications for "sacrifices" our culture makes, willingly but unwittingly.

The next sermon takes as a point of departure Leviticus 19, which thus enjoins the "People of the Covenant": "When you reap the harvest of your land, you shall not reap to the very edges of your field, or gather the gleanings of your harvest. You shall not strip your vineyard bare, or gather the fallen grapes in your vineyard; you shall leave them for the poor and the alien; I am the LORD" (19:9–10).

Listen as the preacher, by means of metaphor, transposes the requirements of neighbor love from an ancient agrarian society into a contemporary quandary over use of natural resources and immigration policy.

HARVESTING TO THE VERY EDGES[4]

What would it look like for us to be faithful to the ancient com-mandment, "You shall not reap to the very edges of your field"? Whatever it looks like, I am fairly certain that I am not very good at it. There is something about my life that always seems to take me right to the edge of whatever I am doing.

In ancient Israel, commandments like this one resulted in a rather enlightened social policy, one that gave the poor and land-less a means of survival with a modicum of dignity. They had a place. It was their right to harvest the edges of the fields that did not belong to them. They were *entitled* to the fallen grapes. It was not charity to leave the edges and the last grapes on the vine; it was a way for the community to define itself as one that provided for all its members, leaving no one out, not even the aliens. That was very important, for remember, the Israelites were once aliens in the land of Egypt.

What would it look like for us not to reap to the edges of our fields or gather the last grapes in our vineyards? We could, I sup-pose, make an immediate leap into the realm of public policy, framing, as one example, the affordable housing initiatives that St. John's and other religious communities have championed in the context of this teaching. For our desire to ensure that all can afford to live in decent homes is not about charity; it is about the kind of people we are and the community we wish to create for future generations. Currently there is a tremendous housing shortage for workers of modest income—the people who care for our children, build our roads, and process our food. Many of the people upon whose labors our lives depend simply cannot afford to live in our communities. Why is that? Perhaps because as a society, we tend to harvest to the very edges of our fields. We take the last grapes for ourselves, so that there is nothing to spare.

Such a teaching also calls to mind the way we treat the aliens in our midst. What part of our fields and vineyards belongs to them? After all, they are the ones who actually *harvest* our fields and vineyards. Undocumented workers also wash our dishes when we go out to eat. They clean our hotel rooms when we travel. They package the terrible food we eat on airplanes. They empty the bedpans in our hospitals and nursing homes. And they pay taxes on every penny they earn. Most economists agree that if all the undocumented workers in the United States were to return to their native lands tomorrow, we would suffer tremendously. We need these people, and amazingly, we do not even see them, much less acknowledge our debt to them. Our ancestors were once aliens in this land. What does the way we treat undocumented workers say about who we are?

Here connections between different worlds are more immediately obvious. And the questions for discernment, in light of the practices of hospitality and of reverence for creation, are much more directly drawn: What are we doing to others, to the environment, to ourselves, by pushing to the edge of our resources?

The importance of practices for the preacher remains heuristic. Practices offer a means of making sense of our actions by drawing together specific acts in terms of common intentions and opening a conversation regarding what acts are called for in a particular situation. Paraphrasing the anthropologist Clifford Geertz, practices are models of action and models for action.[5] They make sense of what we have done and point to what needs to be done. But this only happens in the concrete. We seek to make sense of things when they are called into question. We explore what to do when all is not clear. So the preacher has the opportunity to raise the quandaries that confront or threaten us in order to explore how God is present and how we are to respond. In this way the direction preaching moral discernment offers is inseparable from exploring and ultimately proclaiming how God is with us and ultimately saves us.

Explorations in moral discernment are themselves always communal. The actions and voices of others call our world into question and call for our response. Further, we discern what is happening and what are the possibilities for the future only as we listen to others. We need a community that serves as a community of moral discernment as well as a community of support. For Christians that is the church, the body of Christ.

Preaching moral discernment is not then narrowly focused on the individual but on forming a community of moral discernment. The conversation in the pulpit must take root in the congregation. This brings us to the opportunity offered by the Epistles as they are narratives of communal discernment.

Notes

1. This sermon was preached by David Schlafer at Christ Church, Alexandria, Virginia, on September 23, 2001 and published in *The Journal of the College of Preachers* (England) 112 (January 2002): 7–12, and subsequently in *Preaching Through Holy Days and Holidays: Sermons That Work XI*, ed. Roger Alling and David J. Schlafer (Harrisburg, PA: Morehouse Publishing, 2003), 83–87.

2. This sermon was preached by Anne Howard at Trinity Church, Santa Barbara, California, on September 11, 2005.

3. This sermon was preached by Susan Gaumer at St. Andrew's Church, New Orleans, Louisiana, on March 12, 2006.

4. This sermon was preached by Marianne Budde on May 13, 2001, at the Church of St. John the Baptist in Minneapolis, MN, and published in the *Virginia Seminary Journal* (July 2002): 43–46.

5. Clifford Geertz, "Religion as a Cultural System," in *The Interpretation of Cultures: Selected Essays* (New York: Basic Books, 1973), 118.

CHAPTER 8

Narratives of
Communal Discernment

SOME YEARS AGO, Donald Coggan, late Archbishop of Canterbury, articulated his theology of proclamation in *Preaching: The Sacrament of the Word*.[1] The words of the preaching event are to the Word made flesh, said Coggan, as the bread and wine of the altar are to the body and blood of the Christ. Bread, wine, and word—all offered to God, and, through God's gracious action, become means of grace, manifestations of Christ's real presence in our lives. The words of the one who presides at Communion are not an incantation but the expression of a community's offering. Similarly, a preacher's words are not infusions from a privileged position, but means by which congregations are convened in Spirit-ed conversation.

An effectively delivered sermon is not a dispatch, a "drop-off." It may sound like a monologue, but when a sermon "really works" it unfolds as a network of interchanges. The preacher's word evokes responses that cascade into overt dialogue, both within the liturgy proper and beyond it.

Sermons are *concentrated conversations*, orchestrating all the voices to which preachers have been listening. Good sermons don't reiterate such conversations, they regenerate them. They do not come to a "dead stop" when the preacher concludes but catalyze further conversations that contribute to the process of transformation they intend.[2]

If this is true of preaching generally, it is particularly so when the primary purpose is moral discernment. As we have argued throughout, discernment cannot be "pronounced"; it must be sparked and stirred. Even if preachers have "answers," their task is not to hand them down but to shape a space in which community members can deliberate, discover, draw conclusions, and undertake implementation themselves. What better could be said of those who seek to preach what Christians practice than that they were able to foster conversations through which their community discerned courses of faithful action the preacher never envisioned?

It is helpful to consider the genre of Epistle literature in this light. These are letters, of course, but in their received form—particularly as promulgated in the lectionary—they are often treated as (1) a set of theological principles (somewhat abstractly formulated), (2) a list of moral injunctions (the "application" of said principles), and (3) a smattering of personal reflections (anachronisms in our ears—ramblings, even). In short, what makes our eyes glaze over (and what our preachers skip over).

But what if preachers heard the Epistle authors as colleagues in the task of preaching moral formation and discernment? Suppose, with a combination of close reading and the resources available from current biblical scholarship, we were able to employ Epistle texts as frames of reference for moral formation and decision? Suppose these texts, at least in many cases, are an interplay between narratives of salvation history and narratives of communal discernment?

In some cases—for example, concerning whom we welcome into fellowship in the household of faith, and how—we may find clear resonance between discernment struggles in early Christian communities and those we now encounter. In other cases, what may engage our attention are the strategies employed by Epistle authors in their efforts toward moral mentoring. How they go about fostering formation and discernment may be as or more important than what the letter is supposedly "about" (e.g. "law and grace," "faith, hope, and love," "circumcision," "meat offered to idols"). And if we read these letters from the perspective of

Scripture as a whole, we find them in dialogue with other texts that bring still further voices to the conversation, and so together facilitate our moral discernment processes.

The book of Acts (particularly in the early chapters) prefigures such discernment as it gives us dramatic vignettes of Christians struggling (at no small risk) over what particular forms worship and forgiveness, householding and hospitality should take:

- The "sharing of possession" stories of Barnabas, Ananias and Sapphira (4:32–5:11).

- The contention regarding food distribution to Hellenistic widows, and its resolution in the appointment of "The Seven" (6:1–7).

- Philip's decision, without explicit apostolic warrant, to baptize the Ethiopian eunuch with whom he had just been discussing the text of Isaiah (8:26–40).

- The engaging of Saul (persecutor suddenly presenting as convert) by another Ananias, Damascus believers, and Barnabas (9:10–31).

- Peter's noonday vision, followed by his visit with Cornelius, and then by his defense in Jerusalem about eating with uncircumcised Romans (10–11:18).

- The Jerusalem Council meeting and its deliberations over whether Gentiles were to be welcomed into the body of Christ without first becoming Jews (15:1–41).

Acts 15, in fact, depicts in detail a tense, extended encounter in which there was "no small dissension and debate" (15:2). The author we designate "Luke" palpably depicts the fledgling church trying to deal with issues previously engaged but largely deferred until a moral quandary (how requirements of householding could be reconciled with those of hospitality) comes to a crisis point. This well-known account is as important for the process it describes as for the decision it records. Acts 15 serves as a model for moral discernment in Christian communities.[3]

Luke's Paul manifests "sermon as Spirit-ed conversation" elements in his encounters at Phillipi, Athens, Jerusalem, and

Caesarea (chapters 16, 17, 21–22, and 24, respectively). In his own writings Paul makes use of similar strategies, strategies we can lose sight of if we approach his letters totally focused on the theological themes we take to be his "themes." Passionate, opinionated, polemical Paul can surely be. In his letters, however, Paul is not trying to land crushing blows on his theological adversaries or to dazzle his intended audience with rhetorical brilliance. Above all, he is trying to shape in his listeners a frame of reference for contending with difficult moral quandaries. In their own ways, so are other Epistle authors.

This is not to deny the theological richness of the Epistles nor to imply that reading them through a "moral discernment in moral crisis" lens is the only or necessarily preferred reading. What we are suggesting, however, is that moral discernment is an essential character of the Epistles. They are not narrowly treatises on "salvation by grace through faith," "kenosis," or "logos Christology"—with moral exhortations attached. Instead, the Epistles need to be heard as "narratives of communal moral discernment."

- Romans is about "salvation by grace through faith" and "presenting [our] bodies as a living sacrifice." But it is also Paul's attempt to help a community negotiate its way toward its corporate vocation when the respective theological and moral credentials of Jew and of Gentile are regarded with skepticism by the other party.

- The Corinthian correspondence is about "love," "resurrection," "many members in one body," and "apostolic authority." It is also seeks to discern a vision of corporate Christian living to bear on patterns of power politics, economic inequity, and social discrimination.

- Galatians is a ringing call to freedom in Christ; it is also freedom fostered by disciplined moral formation that cultivates "the fruits of the spirit."

- Philippians is about a self-emptying Christ whom God has exalted and about the possibility of joy in the face of adversity; it also concerns faithful folk who have had a falling out.

- Ephesians and Colossians are about High Christology and claiming citizenship in heaven; they also seek to bear responsible witness in a first-century social order.

- Hebrews paints a panoramic vision of a Great High Priest who is nonetheless able to sympathize with human weaknesses; it also strives to empower the church to undertake practical strategies of mutual love, many specifically addressed to the needs of those who themselves suffer "outside the camp."

- The Pastoral Epistles depict the Christian vocation as "God's own people" who are called to "proclaim the mighty acts of him who called [them] out of darkness into his marvelous light" (1 Pet 2:9); they also press readers of the early church to deal with details of both householding and citizenship.

Part of the difficulty in accessing the energy of Epistle texts involves how they appear in the lectionary (or don't). The adventure in discernment on which Epistle authors seek to lead their listeners often spans much, if not all, of the letter. An oral reading of extended sections would usually require inordinate service time in regular worship: a length far exceeding the attention spans of most contemporary listeners. On Sunday mornings, therefore, congregations hear what lectionary framers have deemed a letter's "high points" of doctrine or exhortation. If, however, Epistles can be understood as narratives of communal discernment, then to hear excerpts only is, inevitably, to miss out on the story, the "big picture," the unfolding of the argument.

While sermon series on the Epistles are sometimes presented, the effect (whether intended or not) is usually one of didactic summation—again, hardly a mimetic enactment of the narrative itself. And few preachers can count on a consistently present congregation "tracking" with them, week after week for the duration. Thus it is important for preachers to steep themselves in the discernment drama unfolding across the entire piece of correspondence; and in individual sermons to "play," as is appropriate to each particular sermon plot, what is at issue and at stake for listeners, both original and contemporary.

What might that look like, for different Epistles, with different moral practice lenses, with different preaching strategies designed to draw listeners into conversation? While there is not space enough or time to offer full sermon illustrations of the many variables we have considered, here, at least are some "prompts," some indications of possible directions.

CONVENING A DISCERNMENT CONVERSATION REGARDING RECONCILIATION

The irony (and often the tragedy) in the work of reconciliation is that urgent calls for it sound irrelevant until they are needed, and then they seldom work! Even the notion of convening a fruitful conversation on reconciliation is problematic. Genuine conversation tends to shut down when fault lines develop within communities, each side holding fast to a "truth" deemed incompatible with the other's "truth." Paul faces such a situation in the congregation at Philippi. A rift has developed. Two prominent participants have fallen out (each probably surrounded by supporters).

Paul addresses the conflict in Philippi by means of indirection, confronting it without being confrontational, weaving words of healing grace back and forth across a broader theological tapestry, slowly but deftly bringing everyone on board, painstakingly marking out the common ground on which all stand, even though they seem oblivious to the fact.

- "I am confident of this, that the one who began a good work among you will bring it to completion by the day of Jesus Christ" (Phil 1:6), he says in an opening doxology, having noted how the community has been continually "sharing in the gospel."
- Sketching the challenges he faces, Paul expresses his desire to visit them, encouraging them (as a seeming aside) to live lives "worthy of the gospel" so that, even if he only gets reports second hand, he will know they are "standing firm in one spirit, striving side by side with one mind for the faith of the gospel" (1:27).

- Warming to his theme (and playing several variations), he sings a song of high and humble Christology: their *same* mind will be engendered by letting *this* mind be in them which was in Christ Jesus (2:1–10).

- This saving mindset, he continues, is a treasure they must steward "with fear and trembling"—not because they are under threat, but because they have been touched where they live with power from on high (2:12–16).

- By means of spiritual autobiography, Paul illustrates what is entailed in Christ-like humility, its costs, its challenges (chapter 3).

- Naming the primary parties in conflict, he urges them to be "of the same mind," invoking the aid of the community in the work of reconciliation (4:1–3).

- "Finally" (having signaled its importance before), Paul sweeps the community into sheer rejoicing, then gives some practical advice about staying centered in doxology: look for, and name in each other, whatever is true, honorable, just, pure, pleasing, commendable, excellent, and worthy of praise (4:4–9).

- He thanks them for their generosity and registers his trust that God will provide for their needs (4:19).

What might we appropriate from Paul about convening conversations concerning reconciliation when the issue cannot be swept under the rug just by "making nice" or asking rhetorically, "Can't we all just get along?"

- Identify, fissures notwithstanding, common values and commitments.

- Depict an undergirding theological frame of reference—preferably in ways that "sing" rather than expound—ways that engender imagination, that call forth prayer and worship, not just discussion and debate.

- Remind all concerned that hard questions must be "worked out with fear and trembling," since what is at stake in how the issue is addressed is of greater concern than the issue itself.

- Make liberal use of engaging case studies in spiritual cost, conflict, and challenge.

- Address specifics even-handedly, non-judgmentally, communally.

- Provide focus for continuing interchange, through appreciative truth-telling rather than polemical mud-slinging.

- Affirm the centrality of prayer and worship as a wellspring of spiritual energy for the work of reconciliation.

Paul does not toss out these strategies indiscriminately. He carefully plots them in tension/*telos* interplay. Contemporary preachers cannot simply mimic that, but they can creatively emulate it. In other words, Paul's preaching *form* may be as or more relevant in preaching toward discernment as his *content*—especially because we are not even told what the conflict in the church at Philippi entailed.

The challenge of preaching reconciliation, though, involves still more. It is certainly proclaiming and evoking the larger purposes we share, the mind of Christ. It is also more than bearing one another's burdens or coming together to rejoice in the life of faith that we share. These are important, but reconciliation requires more. Reconciliation is needed because something has divided us. Reconciliation does not always mean coming to agreement: an impossibility when consciences are deeply divided. The divide over moral judgments about homosexuality in mainline Protestant churches, for instance, is a given. The quandary is not what to do, but what reconciliation might mean in the face of intractable division. Ways forward may be discerned in the Epistles; behind them stands an understanding of the actions that constitute practice of reconciliation.

So, what if we employed some of Paul's theological and homiletical insights to the sharp divisions Christians currently encounter regarding homosexual orientation, as focused through understanding of what is involved in seeking reconciliation? One way is to approach the issue as a topic (as William Sloan Coffin did with the sermon summarized in chapter 6). But that will neither dissolve all disagreement nor address the estrangement these differences produce. Perhaps another approach might

unfold along the following lines (here summarized not as an outline of points but as a sketch of plot moves in sequence).

1. Have you ever found yourself trying to referee a long-standing
    disagreement between folks whose opposing convictions
    were sincerely and firmly held? Not a spat between greedy
    grandchildren fighting over who inherits what, but a battle
    between self-sacrificing patriots, each with political philoso-
    phies so alien as to envision the demise of the nation at the
    adoption of the other? Talking it out doesn't help; ignoring
    the issue doesn't make it go away; mediation seems impossi-
    ble; and a stand-off on the issue could bring the nation to a
    standstill. That's Paul trying to talk to the Philippians.

2. Such disagreements, especially when acted out destruc-
    tively, seem so pointless. But not if you are one of the dis-
    putants! So much is at stake, and it is virtually impossible "not
    to take it personally." What if we lived in Philippi, your name
    was Euodia, mine was Syntyche, and we had been trying to
    dance our way around whatever it was for years and years?

3. Names and places change; issues do as well. Conflict dynam-
    ics don't. What if Paul found himself trying to referee our
    deep divisions with regard to same-sex marriages: each side
    quoting Scripture at the other, each praying that the other
    side would come to understand that "thy will be done"
    means "my will be done!" What might Paul suggest we do
    when every option for some folks is not an option for others?

4. We gather together (on opposite sides of the room) hoping
    he will set the other side straight, or that he will introduce
    considerations none of us have previously considered (after
    all, we're open-minded). Or maybe we are resigned to hear
    from him what preachers tend to do: shame all sides into
    silent submission.

5. But—what's this! He's starting to sing! And he can barely
    manage to carry a tune! This is embarrassing. This is irrele-
    vant. This is . . . what we deeply know (an utterly lovingly,

condescending Christ), and what we long to be (standing side by side in partnership with the Gospel). But what good? It is theology abstracted from our conflict.

6. Paul nods in recognition to our objection but seems to disregard it. Instead, he motions us to join in singing: first about a humble and exalted Christ, but then about one another! He's singling us out, one after another, for solo parts—but parts in which we are required to sing the virtues of the folks with whom we disagree!

7. Paul probably won't show up in person to host a parish sing-a-long. But suppose that, before we sat down to debate the issue one more time, to take a vote about who, if we split, will end up with what. Suppose we were not allowed to do any of that before we had all been locked up in the church—every last one of us—and not allowed to leave, or even say another word, until we had sung together for a solid hour?

8. And once we have sung—not "sung our hearts out," but sung our way *into* our hearts and closer to the heart of the Self-Emptying One—what will we want, and need, to ask ourselves? Perhaps questions like these:

- How and where have we stood shoulder to shoulder in service of the Gospel? What differences *there* have been engendered by, or might engender, our differences *here*?

- How have we, respectively, found challenge and borne cost in bearing witness to the Gospel through our respective understanding of sexuality as gift and discipline?

- Where, in our own respective attempts to work out our own salvation through advocating and defending, are there reasonable grounds for "fear and trembling"?

- If we separate from one another for the sake of witness to the Gospel or if we stay together for the sake of the Gospel, how will we be with one another? Can we respect each other in our differences? What can and should we still do together, just as we may ask that of all who call themselves Christians?

In this particular "take" on Paul's text and this issue, the primary focus of the sermon is to name the moral crisis (as "turning point," not "paroxysm of pain") by means of images (see chapter 6). Such moral discernment includes framing the crisis differently, theologically, and naming courses of action that suggest what reconciliation might look like.

CONVENING A CONVERSATION DISCERNING CARE FOR THE ELDERLY

The Corinthian correspondence offers another example of possibilities for preaching moral discernment through the Epistles. At first, the two letters to Corinth can seem like a motley assortment of strange topics (food sacrificed to idols, head coverings for women, litigation in secular courts, table manners at the Lord's Supper) and less than helpful platitudes ("love is patient, love is kind"). More, though, is going on.

Just because one possesses strong opinions and powerful rhetoric, says Paul, it does not follow that one has the mind of Christ. If so-called "knowledge" generates fragmentation, polarization, power plays, and further benefits for the already privileged at the expense of those on the margins, its purported claims are suspect. In their enthusiasm for designer-driven spiritual community, Paul asserts, the Corinthians have, again and again, rushed to judgment: pronouncing it "before the time," the time when God "will bring to light the things now hidden in darkness and will disclose the purposes of the heart" (1 Cor 4:5).

The Corinthian correspondence is *all* about moral discernment; the topics Paul addresses are places in their corporate life where a moral searchlight needs to be thrown, deliberately, systematically, sequentially, in the hope that new ways of looking at things will happen, new possibilities will be discerned.

As in the letter to the church at Philippi, Paul announces his focus deftly, giving thanks that God has enriched them "in speech and knowledge of every kind," so that they "are not lacking in any spiritual gift": gifts with which God will "strengthen [them] to the end, so that [they] may be blameless on the day of our

Lord Jesus Christ (1 Cor 1:4–8). *That* day, however, is not *this* day; so Paul presents a searching diagnosis of the crippling effects on the household of God being wreaked by individualistic intelligence undertaken "without discerning the body."

Paul supplements his image of a living organism comprised of mutually interdependent parts with images drawn from agriculture and building construction (1 Cor 3:1–17). Any moral discernment that does not contribute to the constituting of a healthy household is foolishness, no matter how wise it seems. If the community is so preoccupied with political positioning that it cannot fulfill its pledge toward famine relief in Jerusalem (2 Cor 8–9) or treat with respect the needy who show up for their own Communion services (1 Cor 11), then the "knowledge" they possess is morally bankrupt.

Do Paul's words have any relevance for moral discernment in the Christian community regarding quandaries concerning the sanctity of life, reproductive choices, and patterns of consumption? As a direct answer, obviously not; but they do "focus attention," both serving as "a reminder that life is given through a set of actions that open and sustain what is the divine economy," and, as such, "a counter to the contemporary ethic of individualistic self-fulfillment" (chapter 4). How one might regard abortion on demand, for example, seen in Pauline perspective, might be different than what one might think about the moral legitimacy of certain forms of stem cell research.

These Pauline texts, in other words, do not speak *about* every issue we face regarding householding and hospitality. But the dialogue of which we have been speaking (between the narratives of Scripture and the narratives of experience, quandaries and practices, narratives of salvation history and narratives of discernment) is precisely, we believe, what constitutes faithful preaching—the kind from which people can not stay away. So, for one example among many, how might Paul's discernment narrative regarding wisdom, played through his image of members of the body, shed light on a question that haunts a great many of us: what responsibility do we have, as individuals and as a society, to care for the elderly and infirm?

1. Are you old enough to remember the TV series *Father Knows Best*? Life was good, issues were straightforward, and "Father's" wise word was benevolent law: an unfailing diagnosis and prescription for every adolescent growing pain. How quickly culture shifts and perceptions change. Seldom, now, do parents command such respect; and seldom do they possess such answers.

2. Nowhere is that more evident than in complex issues surrounding health care and the choices regarding investments of time, money, and personal attention with aging parents and the elderly. How do we spend the lives we have? How do we invest that expenditure in lives of those we love, and those we don't know?

3. So much of our choosing is driven by assessments of cost and benefit. What goods and services must we cut from some to pay for the needs of others? Do we write a check to the graduate school or the nursing home? Do we spend the afternoon at the soccer field or in the hospital? Do we cut the budget for drug rehabilitation to provide prescription drug benefits for those on social security? How much do we take from Peter in order to pay Paul? What is best—who knows best? Choices require calculations and competent calculators. Number crunching is necessary, but is it sufficient? Efficiency of expenditure is essential, but is efficiency the only measure of good stewardship, particularly when we confront the question, what (or who) is expendable?

4. Paul has a seemingly impractical answer: no one is expendable. Indeed, "the members of the body that seem to be weaker are indispensable" (1 Cor 12:22). That sounds like a monkey wrench tossed into the middle of cost/benefit analysis. Does Paul know best? If so, what does *he* know that *we* need to know?

5. Paul is not throwing calculation to the winds; he is inviting us to revisit our investment strategies. Hard calls have to be

made, of course, but such calls, for members of the body of Christ, must take into account resources that a straight-forward social calculus cannot factor. We have been, he says, enriched "in every way" so that we "are not lacking in any spiritual gift" (1 Cor 1:5, 7). And those gifts are displayed in members of the body who seem least necessary since they render it most vulnerable.

6. What would it mean, in decisions regarding care for the elderly, the physically weak (and for others at risk), to ask not, "What can we afford?" but instead ask, "What must we remember about how we are connected? How do we listen and help those in need hear that we are listening? How do we respect their choices and not impose ours? How can we tell the truth and name the possibilities, the choices, the inevitable losses?"

7. There are no "Father knows best" answers to which we can revert in addressing matters of death and dying and care for those in need. But what if the context for such decision-making were to shift from "What shall we do?" to "How do we give thanks, commending ourselves to God"?

In this "trial run," the shaping rhetorical element is argument, by means of which listeners are invited "into reflective analyses concerning the meanings and implications of Christian practices" (chapter 7). This sermon plot attempts to "set forth a case," by means of drawing an analogy between "members of the body" in ancient Corinth and in a contemporary setting characterized by an increasingly aging population

CONVENING A DISCERNMENT CONVERSATION CONCERNING IMMIGRATION POLICY

One more example follows, drawing on familiar Epistle passages that seem to speak clearly regarding Christians' responsibility in the political order.

The author of 1 Peter takes what is often regarded as an authoritarian approach to social arrangements at several levels: Citizens, submit to the emperor. Slaves, submit to masters. Wives, submit to husbands. Taken out of context as abstract injunctions, each of these can be highly problematic. Once again, however, these moral injunctions sound different when set in the context of the narrative of discernment unfolded across the letter and in conversation with the whole of the New Testament.[4]

The challenge of engaging those within the household and those beyond its doorway is framed in the context of being "a chosen race, a royal priesthood, a holy nation, God's own people, in order that you may proclaim the mighty acts of him who called you out of darkness into his marvelous light" (1 Peter 2:9). Membership in such a realm inevitably involves being "aliens and exiles" (1 Peter 1:17; 2:11) in relationship to the powers that be. This requires bearing clear witness to another way of being— a different kind of household, the household of God. Such witness will inevitably lead to suffering—suffering inflicted by those who do not understand and are threatened by a radically different set of allegiances.

"Suffer you will, but don't die on the wrong hills!" this author seems to say. Meet these strangers at the threshold of your household. By giving no occasion for unnecessary misunderstanding and malicious misrepresentation, you will demonstrate to your unbelieving neighbors where the *real* boundaries are between The One realm and all others.

In other words, discernment, again. And for us, perhaps the continuing dialogue can best be conducted by accepting the premise and questioning the behavioral implications: What does membership in "a holy nation" involve in relation to a nation where the political right claims authoritarian prerogatives as an all but divine right? How much, and what kind of, "submission" and "suffering" are appropriate "trouble" to undertake in our attempts to be hospitable to the stranger?

The letter to the Romans can be seen similarly. If we read Romans 13:1–7 as a stand-alone piece, the requirements of Christian citizenship seem clear: do whatever the government tells you! Set within the larger discernment narrative, however (even if restricted to Romans 12, and the remaining verses of chapter 13), the answer becomes more complex. There is an intriguing tension between the apparent political imperatives of 13:1–5 and the requirements of becoming a "living sacrifice" (12:1): "do not be conformed to this world, but be transformed by the renewing of your minds, so that you may discern what is the will of God" (12:2). Employing these two chapters in such a way as to justify a "two swords" theory of citizenship and political responsibility carves this material up altogether too neatly.

Granted the earnest exhortations to radical discipleship on both sides of the "let every one be subject to the governing authorities" passage, a case can be made for reading those "be subject" verses as meaning that "you've got the Reign of God to embody—so don't get distracted by merely Roman bureaucracy!"

Then there is the conclusion to this "obey the government" section: "Pay to all what is due them—-taxes to whom taxes are due, revenue to whom revenue is due, respect to whom respect is due, honor to whom honor is due" (13:7). But what is that, precisely? If it is a flat pronouncement, it is a mere platitude. But what if it is intended rather as a faith community conversation-starter?

How might this approach to Paul's "theology of citizenship" take form in a sermon sketch that seeks to convene a discernment conversation on immigration policy? Here would be a sermon rhetorically shaped by story, the one Barbara Brown Taylor told us back in chapter 6.

1. "The powers that be are ordained of God!" "The law is the law!" The two phrases are often heard, together, uttered by many God-fearing, law-abiding folks. Those who take church seriously may not be above exceeding the speed limit on occasion, but they pay their fines when they are caught (and even feel good about it).

2. "This is not about discrimination, it's about illegal behavior." One often heard that in the Deep South not too many years

ago. "Civil rights protestors are criminals!" Both phrases, again, spoken by those who went to church: the very ones who uttered the other phrases.

3. How do those sentiments relate to what is often termed "the problem of illegal immigration"? All of a sudden it isn't so clear, because the nation is divided now and not simply along party lines (or even ethnic lines). If "the State" has spoken and we must obey, it's hard to know just what to do; the state sends all sorts of conflicting signals.

4. It is pretty clear that Paul has a respectful view for government, in its proper place. Just what that place might be, however, is not entirely clear. Paul sends conflicting signals as well. He has just been talking to citizens of Rome about the need to "offer themselves as a living sacrifice," the first manifestation of which is not "to be conformed to this world but to be transformed by the renewing of [their] minds." What does such transformation look like on the ground?

5. In ancient Israel strangers were welcomed and were to be released from slavery, but only on the Jubilee, on the Sabbath of Sabbaths, on the fiftieth year. You can't have an economy if there are no terms of exchange. You can't have a nation without boundaries. And yet, illegal immigrants are *resident* aliens. They are already members of our community just like the indentured servants, the slaves, in ancient Israel.

6. As with many thorny social issues our government struggles to address, the presenting problem is the tip of the iceberg. Who we let in, under what conditions, and what we should do with those who haven't followed all the rules—wouldn't it be nice if all we had to do was wait for our Congress to make up its mind and get on with upholding the law! Whatever they managed to come up with, however, is not the voice of God, any more than Caesar's voice was the voice of Paul's Sovereign Lord.

7. How shall we approach those deeper issues? Barbara Brown Taylor recounts an experience that does not give an answer but helps to pose the question.[5]

8. Paul doesn't give us any policy answers, any more that Barbara Taylor's story does. But on both sides of his endorsement of stable government he outlines what such policies would embody: "Live in harmony with one another; do not be haughty, but associate with the lowly; do not claim to be wiser than you are." (In a word, no pecking order politics.) "Love your neighbor as yourself. Love does no wrong to a neighbor; therefore, love is the fulfilling of the law." *That* law *is* the law—and the only one that has divine authority.

While brief images (primarily of verbal sound bites) are employed here, and a process of reasoning is deployed, what makes this sermon "work" is the reframing of the issue by means of the "Guinea Hen" parable. Stories, as we observe in chapter 6, are well-suited for leading listeners into wrestling with moral quandaries. Since narratives are at the heart of our lives, they enable us to entertain alternatives, to switch or change stories.

From the outset we have made a distinction between narratives of salvation history and narratives of communal discernment; and we have pressed—for purposes of moral discernment preaching—the importance of the latter in relation to the former. It will not do, we believe, in preaching the "full Gospel" simply to announce the fact and promise of God's gracious healing for human wounding, set forth in the "sermon as story."

And yet, salvation history has an important place in moral formation preaching. Were it not for God's saving work, there would be no point in preaching Christian moral formation and discernment. Furthermore, salvation history can serve not only as the ground but also as the means for convening a community's conversation regarding moral discernment. And this can be done with striking effectiveness from Epistle as well as Gospel texts.

As you will hear in the sermon that follows, the proclamation of our salvation can raise the sense of crisis posed by the threat of ecological destruction. And that proclamation can also shape a space and set a direction for communal moral discernment about what the practice of reverence for creation means and requires.

AND IN HIM ALL THINGS HOLD TOGETHER[6]
Colossians 1:11–29

When the lectionary stops abruptly mid-thought, the preacher catches her breath with excitement; for she knows that whatever was left out is bound to be troublesome, and for that reason eminently worth preaching. And so it is in this case. The portion of Colossians appointed for the theme "Of the Reign of Christ" stops in the middle of a discussion of how God is reconciling all things to himself through Christ. This morning we overrode the lectionary and let "Paul" finish the thought so we could hear the crucial assurance: "You who were once estranged and hostile in mind," you, too, can be presented holy and blameless before God, "provided that you continue securely established and steadfast in the faith, without shifting from the hope promised by the gospel that you heard, which has been proclaimed to every creature under heaven" (1:23).

"The gospel . . . which has been proclaimed to every creature under heaven"—it is easy to see why the lectionary stops short of that phrase, for it is truly wild. Think about it—"every creature under heaven." If we take that seriously, are we to believe that the Good News is meant not just for "every family, language, people and nation" (Canticle 18, Rev 5:9; cf. Daniel 7:14) but also for rock badgers and rocks, fruit bats and giant sequoias? How can we take that seriously? It sounds flaky; it smacks of animism. Moreover, it is too far from our understanding of the Great Commission. However strong may be our commitment to evangelism, who among us is prepared to answer to giant sequoias for the proclamation of the Gospel?

Yet the whole point of the passage is that human beings cannot be firmly separated off from the rest of the creatures when it comes to the work of God in Christ. In Christ, Paul (or whoever wrote Colossians) tells us "all things in heaven and on earth were created, things visible and invisible," humans and powers of the spirit world, things animate and inanimate. "*All things* have been created through Christ and for Christ . . . and in him *all things* hold together" (1:16–17). "All things," *ta panta*— four times repeated—all things hold together in Christ, and through Christ all things are reconciled to God. I do not pretend to completely understand that; this is mystical insight that reaches beyond my grasp. But this I think is true: Colossians is presenting us with a radical Christology in which doctrine of Christ and doctrine of creation are inextricably intertwined. "He is . . . the firstborn of all creation": incarnation and creation are finally inseparable, and the inclusion of every creature in the evangelical imperative follows from that. Because God made everything *in* Christ and *for* Christ, then it follows that everything needs to hear proclaimed the Good News of Christ, and actively claim its own place in the gospel story.

The creation is, then, a unity. Every creature—every person, every stick and stone and stallion and seahorse—is profoundly related to every other creature. This is the picture with which Colossians presents us. But to us in the twenty-first century, the essential unity of creation does not come as divine revelation. Scientific reports and the popular press have made us painfully aware that all of us on "this small blue dot" share a common fate. If the ship goes down, we all drown—a possibility we cannot discount. The unity of all creatures is something many of us are coming to acknowledge as a fact, and currently it appears to be a fairly grim fact. What difference, then, does the biblical witness make to us in this matter?

This: the letter to the Colossians testifies to the unity of creation *under the universal Lordship of Christ*. It shows us all things held together, not in bondage to a single threatening fate, but all things held together *in Christ*. The difference that biblical faith makes is the difference between accepting a sober fact—our common danger—and accepting an invitation to a party. The Christian participates in the solidarity of the creatures as one who is responding to an invitation to a gala banquet. That is Karl Barth's description of what it means for the Christian to accept the fact that she is a creature, no more and no less, an honored guest of the sovereign Lord of all the worlds. Thus Barth describes the scene in the banqueting hall ". . . there [the Christian] takes his place at the table, in the company of publicans, in the company of beasts and plants and stones, accepting solidarity with them, being present simply as they are, as a creature of God."[7] Christians partying with plants and stones—this is not a vision of the Reign of Christ that our lectionary encourages us to entertain. It backs away from Colossians' testimony that the gospel has indeed "been proclaimed to every creature under heaven." Why are we so reluctant to hear the biblical witness and claim our solidarity with all the creatures of God?

Could it be that we are afraid? Afraid to sit down at the banqueting table and open a conversation with the non-human creatures? Afraid that if we once open that conversation in the presence of God, the other creatures will find their voices, and cry out against us? Afraid that the rivers we have dammed, drained, and poisoned will accuse us of culpable negligence? Afraid that the soil we have stripped of its hardwood forests, the seas we have dragnetted and depopulated will cry out against us for our greed? Afraid that the mountains we are literally taking down to the ground, scraping out veins of low-grade coal and leaving behind vast piles of infertile rubble—are we afraid that the mountains of Kentucky will testify against us, that we have undone the work of God's hands, misused our God-given powers for evil, to satisfy our own selfish whims?

That would be an intelligent fear, well informed not only by modern science and the news media but also, and more significantly, by the Bible, where things that we call "insentient" do, in fact, have a voice. The Prophets appeal to mountains and hills to give witness to the just judgments of the Creator. Then there are those "Fantasia" psalms, that show a fully animated world: the sea shouting, the rivers clapping their hands, the mountains ringing out for joy, for God comes to "judge the world with righteousness, and peoples justly" (Ps 98:9). No wonder they rejoice. God's coming to judge the world is unambiguously Good News for the non-human creatures. For in the Day of Judgment, all creatures will stand in immediate relation to the One who made them. For mountains and rivers, God's judgment means freedom—free at last from our doubtful mercy. The non-human creatures, then, clamor to hear the Good News that our Lord is coming in power and just judgment. No wonder we hesitate to sit at table with them—who wants to be lambasted at dinner? Better to stay away, even if that means missing the meal that God has laid for all the creatures.

But the letter to the Colossians shows us the one condition on which we may come into the banqueting hall without fear of humiliation. We must accept one thing about the rules of this house, namely this: that the wine served here is the blood of sacrifice. Christ's blood poured out for the life of the world is the wine of fellowship that unites all the creatures. In stunning terms, Paul sets forth the sole basis for reconciliation, after all the harm that we have done: ". . . through [Christ] God was pleased to reconcile to himself all things, whether on earth or in heaven, making peace through the blood of the cross" (1:20). "Making peace through the blood of his cross"—those words confound our rationalism, and, if we can hear them, they draw us deep into "the mystery hidden throughout the ages . . . [that] has now been revealed to [the] saints" (26).

Through the blood of the cross. Jesus Christ is healing a breach that dates back nearly to the beginning of world history. The first chapters of Genesis disclose that the dangerous alienation between us and the other creatures originated, not in twentieth-century technology, but rather in the fallout from the first human disobedience. It began as soon as human beings had begun to seek their own way in the world, apart from God. And God said to the snake: "I will put enmity between you and the woman, between your seed and her seed" (Gen 3:15). But now Christ offers to heal that ancient enmity, "making peace through the blood of the cross." From the cross, the center point of all creation, Christ reaches out to embrace all things and reconcile them to God. Christ the Firstborn of all creation, the most privileged of God's children, dying to draw the rest of us back to God—that is an image that has power to heal us from our profound estrangement and hostility of mind, if we can only grasp this one thing: the invitation to the feast of reconciliation is an invitation to sacrifice.

We are invited here, as the liturgy sublimely says, to be united with Christ in his sacrifice.[8] Instructed and emboldened by his sacrifice, we are charged to make our own. Sacrifice—literally "making holy," sanctifying the world by accepting our lives as pure gift and offering back to God any and all of what God has given us. Strange and sad to say, it is easy to miss or misunderstand what the blood of the cross has to teach us about Christian discipleship. The crucial point is this: Christ's sacrifice does not make our sacrifice unnecessary. Rather, his sacrifice makes ours possible. If we are truly united with Christ in his sacrifice, then we are changed, irrevocably, inducted into the strange inverse economics of the kingdom of heaven, where wealth is measured by how much you can afford to do without, comfort level by your ease in giving up.

Sisters and brothers, beloved in the Lord, we are invited now to the feast of reconciliation. If we speak with integrity and eat to our salvation, we commit ourselves to change, *metanoia*, new thought and action, bold and profound. What can we do, what can we give or give up in order that our words and even more our lives may become a genuine and persuasive proclamation of this mystery long hidden that has now been revealed, the mystical solidarity of all creatures, held together in Christ, reconciled to God and one another through the blood of the cross? In our time may that mystical solidarity be made manifest to God's eternal glory, lest we perish in our estrangement. So let us pray for the coming of the reign of Christ:

Almighty and everlasting God, whose will it is to restore all things in your well-beloved Son, the King of kings and Lord of lords: Mercifully grant that the creatures of the earth, divided and enslaved by sin, may be freed and brought together under his most gracious rule: who lives and reigns with you and the Holy Spirit, one God, now and forever.

Notes

1. Donald Coggan, *Preaching: The Sacrament of the Word* (New York: Crossroad, 1988).
2. John S. McClure, *The Roundtable Pulpit: Where Preaching and Leadership Meet* (Nashville: Abingdon Press, 1995); and Lucy A. Rose, *Sharing the Word: Preaching in the Roundtable Church* (Louisville, KY: Westminster John Knox, 1997), explore the role of the congregation in shaping the sermon as well as hearing it. Chapter 8 in David Schlafer's *Playing with Fire: Preaching Work as Kindling Art* (Cambridge, MA: Cowley Publications, 2004), explores this possibility also, as does the whole of Kim Beckmann's *Prepare a Road!*
3. And has direct application for contemporary issues in which there is also "no small dissension and debate"; see, for example, in the Episcopal Church and Anglican Communion, *To Set Our Hope on Christ* (New York: The Episcopal Church Center, 2005).
4. See Carolyn Osiek and David L. Balch, *Families in the New Testament World: Households and House Churches* (Louisville, KY: Westminster/John Knox, 1997).
5. At this point, turn back to the "Guinea Hen" story she tells, which appears in chapter 6, pages 95–96, and, we would suggest, read this story—in its entirety—aloud!
6. This sermon was preached by Ellen Davis in a chapel service at Virginia Theological Seminary, on October 22, 1997, and reprinted in the *Virginia Seminary Journal* (December 1997): 2–5.
7. Karl Barth, *Church Dogmatics*, III/iii (London: T & T Clark, 2004), 242.
8. The Book of Common Prayer, Eucharistic Prayer B.
9. The Book of Common Prayer, 254.

CHAPTER 9

Practicing What We Preach

THE CHALLENGE OF PREACHING MORAL DISCERNMENT, as we have argued, is its many-layered character. We have attempted to capture the multi-dimensional demands of such preaching through the set of six theses we have explored.

- *Thesis 1:* Preaching for moral discernment requires continual interplay between the open-ended narratives of Scripture (where God's actions are proclaimed) and the open-ended narratives of our lives (where God's actions are experienced).

- *Thesis 2:* Preaching moral discernment requires moving away from focusing narrowly on particular issues or narrowly on the Gospels understood primarily as accounts of "saving history."

- *Thesis 3:* Fostering moral discernment and faithful response through preaching also requires moving back and forth between quandaries and practices.

- *Thesis 4:* The Christian moral life is centered in six practices: (1) prayer and worship, (2) forgiveness and reconciliation, (3) the formation of households as communities of faith, (4) hospitality as the embrace of the stranger and those in need, (5) citizenship and political responsibility, and (6) reverence for creation.

- *Thesis 5:* Preaching for moral discernment needs to undertake directly the adventure it seeks to articulate.
- *Thesis 6:* The rhetorical forms of metaphor, narrative, and argument employed in Scripture by "the preachers of the Bible" are the rhetorical forms necessary to effect preaching for moral discernment.

These six theses have their home in the church. As the body of Christ, the church is not a class of students to be taught but a company of persons whose new life is formed together, in communion. This brings us to the last of our seven theses:

- Thesis 7: Preaching toward moral formation requires a community of practices that offers its members clear alternatives to those that are prevailing or taken for granted.

The challenge for communities of faith is that Christian identity is and has always been contested. Since the very beginning, as reflected in the Acts of the Apostles and the Epistles, Christian communities have been marked by what Wayne Meeks calls "a large and often raucous diversity."[1] Paul, therefore, sought to enable discernment in his communities by distinguishing between what he heard as the voice of God and what he regarded as his own judgments. More broadly, the New Testament writings and the Hebrew Scriptures ensured that different voices and judgments were heard as the early Christian community tested the spirits to discern the spirit of God (1 John 4:1).

As the earliest communities of faith discovered, moral discernment is not simply a matter of figuring out what to do. Moral discernment is a matter of seeing and becoming who we are meant to be as Christians. This is variously expressed in Christian tradition. Through our lives we form ourselves as living witnesses of the work of God in Christ (Acts 1:8). We are the body of Christ; in and through us the work of the incarnation goes forward.[2] We are called to holiness, to be sanctified, to live fully in relationship to God. Preaching moral discernment, as evidenced by the earliest narratives of communal discernment, is a matter of discovering, embodying, and proclaiming Christian faith as a new way of life, fully lived in relationship with God.

What we have called moral discernment preaching is not, then, something new. Rather, as in the early church, it is a central task of evangelism and formation. To explore moral crises and choices in terms of the distinctive character of Christian faith is to convey the nature, presence, reality, and grace of God in our lives, and to invite persons into that life. This is a call to conversion.

This understanding of moral discernment as a central task and challenge for preaching is clearly articulated in the liturgical renewal movement.[3] As seen in its origins before Constintine, and in the establishment of Christianity as the religion of the Roman State in 313, the church began as gathered communities who worshipped God and formed their life as distinct from the prevailing culture. Initiation into this new life was central to the church, and with that, the importance of an initiation process (catechumenate).

Baptized into Christ, the church's central expression of life in Christ was the celebration of the Eucharist, the enactment of Jesus' command to "do this in remembrance of me" (1 Cor 11:24–25). Worship was not something done to the people but rather a central practice of Christian persons. Faith required participation in the community of faith so that individuals could be formed together as Christ's own. The liturgical renewal movement, therefore, has emphasized worship in the language of the people (the vernacular), music performed by—not for—the congregation, and congregational participation in the reading of Scripture, the prayers of the people, and the administration of the Eucharist.

This renewal of liturgy—from something done to the worshipper to something that worshippers do as the celebration and deepening of Christian faith—has been paralleled by a renewal of preaching so "that a community of believers who have gathered to celebrate the liturgy may do so more deeply and more fully—more faithfully—and thus be formed for Christian witness in the world." Since Christian faith is given as a life lived in Christ, "what the Word of God offers us is a way to interpret our human lives, a way to face the ambiguities and challenges of the human condition, not a pat answer to every problem and question that comes along."[4] In preaching moral discernment the goal is just that: to effect and deepen Christian faith in response to the world through concrete wrestling with the crises and quandaries we encounter.

As envisioned in the liturgical renewal movement and in other contemporary strategies for preaching, such as narrative preaching, preaching moral discernment assumes a fundamental shift in understanding regarding the authority of the preacher.[5]

For most of Christian history, human communities assumed a corporate identity where a leader spoke to and for the community. Persons became community leaders because of the gifts they evidenced, the social status they enjoyed, or the process of authorization they had undergone. In Christian communities this devolved to the ordained: bishop, priest, and deacon—in that order. By virtue of their education these leaders were able to read Scripture to their communities, most of whom were illiterate. By ordination they were given distinctive powers, especially to baptize, consecrate, and pronounce absolution of sin. The ordained—bishops initially, and then priests (as bishops assumed broader oversight for many congregations)—were ideally the first citizens, those who represented the wisdom of the community and gave their lives to its service. Such was the traditional hierarchy of authority, essentially a "command and obey" model. In this model, the preacher was to present the truth of the Gospel and offer clear pastoral direction to his congregation (and it was a man).

The shift in authority has been ushered in by the Enlightenment and other sweeping changes that have brought us to the twenty-first century. Science, education, communications, competing claims and counterclaims—these question traditional authority. Credibility rests upon making sense of things, not on a leader saying something is so. The preacher's authority is not now taken for granted but is granted in response to his or her ability to convey claims about God, to make connections, and to draw out implications. Christian moral discernment is thus effected by a reframing of what is happening and what possibilities for action might deepen life in Christ.[6] Such discernment may begin with how we make decisions, for example, by exploring how prayer functions in the community's testing of spirits (1 John 4:1). It extends to exploring the larger context of the crises we confront and the purpose God has for our lives.

To speak with authority by making sense of things in light of Christian faith requires a community of faith that practices what it preaches. Without an actual community of faith that lives out Christian faith in distinct practices, there is no reference point, no reality check that marks and mediates faith itself. This is the reason we speak of the church as the body of Christ, God's presence in the world. Without reference to an actual community, preaching can at the most gesture toward a way of life that would be countercultural. Without the community there is no reality that incarnates and makes visible what preaching seeks to articulate.

Liturgical theologians say that Baptism and the Eucharist are sacramental because they "effect what they signify." They signify the action of the community: what the community is indicating (and thereby effecting), just as a kiss expresses, actualizes, and deepens love between two persons. Similarly, preaching changes lives only when it, too, names the reality of life in Christ that is being lived. Named, persons can turn and enter into a new life, but only when that life is palpable. This is why the early church engaged in a strong catechumenal process. Now, as Christian faith again stands in deep contrast to the individualism and consumerism of the present age, a catechumenal process is essential in order to initiate would-be Christians into a community of Christian practice and to deepen the faith of those who have already entered into that community. Without such a life, preaching is impotent.

Still, the specific challenges we have explored remain. First, discerning the crises and choices we confront in light of Christian faith requires a vision of the Christian life. More specifically, as we have said, preachers must have an account of the practices of Christian faith. These practices serve as lenses to focus our attention on what is essential in order to enter and deepen our relationship with God. Practices raise questions and enable persons to identify quandaries they should confront: when to pray, what to pray, why to pray; who to forgive and how to forgive; what to do or not to do in shaping our households and welcoming strangers; what, as God's own, we owe as citizens of the state; and how we honor nature as God's creation.

By identifying actions fundamental to Christian faith, practices often reframe questions by pointing to more basic crises (as turning points) and by offering a perspective that changes the sense of what matters in our response. For example, we react to terrorist attacks with fear, but are called to pray, and so come to hear and see what is happening in a different light. Our households are part of a divine economy, so we value our customs but no longer see them as universal truths. We realize that hospitality to the stranger is the welcoming of God into our lives and apprehend things differently through the eyes of another.

The six practices we have claimed as central to Christian faith offer an account that can then be developed in various ways, given particular traditions and understandings. What makes this so challenging is that, while practices draw together particular actions in terms of broader, common intentions or purposes, only in those particulars does the account become concrete. The vision of the Christian life in terms of the practices of faith thus requires the ongoing study of the history of actual Christian practices.

It is essential that preachers have a clear vision they can articulate in terms of a limited number of practices. More than six threatens to exchange a (re)memorable, integrated account for an extended list of particulars that overwhelm our capacity to see the forest through the trees. To develop an adequate, useful account of Christian practices requires ongoing reading of the Christian tradition, not narrowly as a matter of belief (doctrine) but broadly as a matter of a way of life, what has traditionally been called piety. This means engaging ascetics, mystics, pietists, prophets, and social activists, traditions of oppression and liberation, Anabaptists, Pentecostals, Roman Catholics, Protestants, Orthodox, Anglicans: all these categories themselves drawing together particular figures, each with their own distinct accounts. All can't be studied, but reading both inside and outside one's own tradition is essential.

An account of Christian practices serves as a means of preaching assessment. Preachers do well to review sermons they have preached over the last year to see what they have addressed (and haven't). From our experience we are willing to bet that, in a year, most preachers address only two or three of these practices (most likely prayer and worship, forgiveness and reconciliation, and hospitality). Less addressed (in all likelihood) are quandaries and issues that may be construed in terms of householding, citizenship, and especially reverence for creation.

There are other purposes in preaching, of course, but failure to explore the quandaries posed and the way of life envisioned in terms of each of these practices is a failure to proclaim a fully embodied Christian faith. This further suggests the need to look at lectionary readings during ordinary time (the seasons of Epiphany and Pentecost, as distinct from the cycle of readings for Advent and Christmas, and for Lent and Easter). Of particular importance is attending to the development and range of readings across the seasons of Epiphany and Pentecost as a whole. Only in this way is it possible to move from ad hoc preaching to the comprehensive kind that addresses the crises and quandaries pressing upon us. Not everything can be done in a season or a year, but over time the breadth of Christian practices can be addressed.

A second challenge in preaching moral discernment is developing broad knowledge of crises and quandaries we confront. Moral judgments are not enough. The war on terrorism as defined by George W. Bush may or may not be right. Treating AIDS, ending poverty, immigration reform, and saving the environment are worthy goals. But moral discernment requires understanding the options, the causes or underlying issues, the reasons for conflict, the consequences, trade-offs, and impediments for effective action.

Understanding crises and quandaries can seem like an impossible task. This is surely so if preachers think they must be experts. That, however, presupposes that preachers should offer definitive judgments. Instead, the proclamation of the Gospel in preaching moral discernment comes through seeing a quandary and the broader crisis in terms of Christian faith, and asking new questions about what is happening, seeing possible responses from fresh perspectives, and raising questions about how we might respond so as to witness and deepen our relationship with God.

Why do we have children, and so, should we consider adoption before seeking artificial insemination by a donor? What is health? What is the purpose of medical treatment? When should we discontinue medical treatment at the end of life? What are the limits of the state? What, then, is the justifiable use of force against possible terrorists? What is the place of prayer? How, then, is prayer related to justice and reconciliation?

Commentaries on the lectionary have been largely unhelpful in connecting Scripture to crises and quandaries. They generally confine themselves to conversations between preaching and biblical exegesis, often assuming or implying that preaching is only about proclaiming God's mighty acts in history, and that preaching is the bridge between text and context.[7] A broader conception of a lectionary commentary is needed in order to support preaching moral discernment.

Exegesis is certainly important for understanding a text. Preaching moral discernment, however, also requires the exploration of moral discernment in Scripture—both in specific texts, and more broadly in the conversation between texts. A commentary commencing such a conversation would, no doubt, be far more particular than traditional commentaries, but that is part of the problem of traditional commentaries.

Finally, preaching moral discernment requires a community of moral discernment. Sermons are too short and too infrequent to bear the full weight of moral discernment, just as they cannot bear all the weight of providing comfort in distress, or of teaching Scripture and the story of faith. Preaching moral discernment should raise questions and engage individuals in what are the distinctive and compelling claims about our lives as faithful Christians, but it cannot stop there. Preaching discernment must continue in the formation of a community of discernment.

If the congregation is to incarnate Christian faith, then the members of the congregation must themselves be involved in moral discernment. Prayer, forums, and study groups offer opportunities for this. Discernment is grounded in prayer, requires basic knowledge, and happens when we see things from the perspective of others. Christian communities that practice the faith that is preached are communities where people gather together, face-to-face, pray together, listen and learn, test the spirits, and discern what God is calling them to do and to become.

The challenge from the beginning of Christianity has been the assimilation of Christ to culture.[8] The individualism and consumerism of our present age stand in such contrast to the witnesses of Scripture that ours is an age of evangelism not unlike that of the early church.

Our time, though, is also unique. For the first time in history, humans have the power to destroy creation itself, first with the development of the atomic bomb and now in the power to destroy nature. Power evident in the technologies that shape our daily lives continues to offer cure and comfort. Yet as it transforms our lives, it continues to transform our sense of place in the world. Power to determine becomes paramount, and the self takes center stage. Too easily we forget our dependencies and the goodness and glory that stand beyond our lives. Only by heightening consciousness of the quandaries of our lives can we see the crises that we confront daily. As pain and turning point, crises are the necessary condition for conversion to a new life, to life in God. Leading us into and through such crises requires moral discernment. This is the outstanding challenge for preaching in our time.

Notes

1. Wayne A. Meeks, *The Origins of Christian Morality* (New Haven, CT: Yale, 1993), 217.
2. This quote variously attributed to Augustine appears to be a paraphrase of his Eucharistic theology expressed in Sermon 272. See *The Works of Saint Augustine: A Translation for the 21st Century*, ed. John E. Rotelle,

O.S.A., trans. Edmund Hill, O.P. (New Rochelle, NY: New City Press, 1993), III/7, 300–301.

3. On the liturgical movement, see Keith F. Pecklers and Bryan D. Spinks, "The Liturgical Movement," in *The New Westminster Dictionary of Liturgy and Worship*, ed. Paul Bardshaw (Louisville, KY: Westminster John Knox, 2002), 283–89. On the liturgical movement and preaching, see O. C. Edwards, Jr., *A History of Preaching* (Nashville, TN: Abingdon, 2004), 688–702.

4. Bishop's Committee on Priestly Life and Ministry of the U.S. Conference of Catholic Bishops, *Fulfilled in Your Hearing: The Homily in the Sunday Assembly* (Washington, DC: U.S. Conference of Catholic Bishops, 1982), 18, 15, as quoted in Edwards, *A History of Preaching*, 694. As noted by Edwards, the primary author of this text was William Skudlarek, O.S.B., and author of *The Word in Worship: Preaching in a Liturgical Context* (Nashville, TN: Abingdon, 1981).

5. See Fred Craddock, *As One Without Authority*, 3rd ed. (Nashville, TN: Abingdon, 1978).

6. On this change in traditional African societies, see Simon E. Chiwanga, "Beyond the Monarch/Chief: Reconsidering Episcopacy in Africa," in *Beyond Colonial Anglicanism*, ed. Ian T. Douglas and Kwok Pui-Lan (New York: Church Publishing, 2001), 297–317.

7. See Edwards, *A History of Preaching*, 677–87. See thesis 1 above, chapter 2.

8. See H. Richard Niebuhr's classic study, *Christ and Culture* (New York: Harper & Row, 1951; repr. 2001, intro. by James Gustafson).

General Index

Scripture Index